CLASSIC
AIRPLANES

PIONEERING AIRCRAFT AND THE VISIONARIES WHO BUILT THEM

C L A S S I C
AIRPLANES

PIONEERING AIRCRAFT AND THE VISIONARIES WHO BUILT THEM

HAROLD RABINOWITZ

MetroBooks

MetroBooks

An Imprint of Friedman/Fairfax Publishers

Library of Congress Cataloging-in-Publication Data

Rabinowitz, Harold, date
    Classic airplanes : pioneering aircraft and the visionaries
    who built them / Harold Rabinowitz.
        p.   cm.
    Includes bibliographical references and index.
    ISBN 1-56799-430-X
    1. Airplanes—History.   I. Title.
TL670.3R33   1997
629.13'009- -dc21   96-37613

Editor: Tony Burgess
Art Director: Kevin Ullrich
Photography Editor: Deidra Gorgos
Production Manager: Jeanne E. Hutter

Color separations by HBM Print Ltd.
Printed in the United Kingdom by Butler & Tanner Limited
1 3 5 7 9 10 8 6 4 2

For bulk purchases and special sales, please contact:
Friedman/Fairfax Publishers
Attention: Sales Department
15 West 26th Street
New York, NY 10010
212/685-6610 FAX 212/685-1307

Visit our website:
http://www.metrobooks.com

Dedication

To Louis Roth, z.l., who flew solo.

Acknowledgments

The path that has led me into the history of aviation and made it a con-suming passion began years ago with the realization that no student of physics had any excuse for not being immersed, or at least versed, in aeronautical science. The books that served as my foundation are listed in the bibliographies of this and my previous book, *Conquer the Sky*, though the debt that I owe Professor John D. Anderson is particularly great. It was my good fortune to work with him and with other histori-ans and practitioners of aeronautical science over the past decade or so, and I am grateful for having had that opportunity (and for having had the good sense to concoct reasonable excuses for working with such people). I single out three in particular: Tom Crouch of the Smithsonian Institution, Jan Roskam of Kansas State University, and Barnes McCormick of Pennsylvania State University. It has been a privilege to work with these people, and I sincerely hope they have not yet had their fill of me.

My editor at Michael Friedman Publishing, Tony Burgess, has been a rock and an inspiration, and I am very appreciative that it has been his deft but firm hand that has shaped this work. The design expertise of Kevin Ullrich and the photo editing of Deidra Gorgos have made this a better book than I deserve, and I join readers in thanking them for their dedication and for applying their considerable talents to the work.

Finally, I thank my wife Ilana and my son Daniel for their support, their patience, and their assistance, even after it became clear that this was not just a passing phase.

Contents

Introduction

What makes a plane great, a classic? There may not be any way to answer that question objectively; if there were, all aircraft would be great and no one would manufacture anything else. It is certainly not a matter of numbers. The performance parameters of an aircraft may provide some clues as to its quality, but in the final analysis, there are many intangibles and imponderables that go into determining greatness for an aircraft. The presence of money, expertise, talented designers, and advanced technology does not guarantee that the result will be a great plane; indeed, these factors do not even guarantee that the product will ever get off the ground, or stay aloft if it does. As in many areas of life, an aircraft needs luck if it is going to rise above the commonplace and become exceptional.

The situation is not so very different with motion pictures (and I am not the first to point out that it is no accident that both the aviation industry and the film industry found the West Coast of the United States a congenial setting). The presence of big stars, great directors, big budgets, and major studio backing still results—surprisingly often—in bombs that lose millions. One stares up—whether at the screen or at the aircraft—and wonders, "What were they thinking?" Given the huge amounts of resources and coordinated effort that go into creating a movie or an airplane, there are many opportunities for wrong turns and misguided decisions, and sometimes the very gravity of the enterprise can addle even the most talented and sure-handed, leading them astray.

But sometimes everything works and comes together, and the result is breathtaking. All the parts fit smoothly, and one can sense that one is in the presence of something great—a classic.

The planes selected for this book all have that quality. There may have been others that performed better, but when they came on the scene the path had already been broken by these classics. Other planes may have represented important improvements and advances, but they provided no surprises, set no new standard against which other planes would thenceforth be measured. If a great plane is missing from this book, the reason is that the innovation that made it great had already been demonstrated by a plane with no ancestry to lean on.

This brings us to the people who make the planes. They are a breed apart. Great planes have their own personalities, and that's because the designers, manufacturers, test pilots, and fliers of great planes are such extraordinary personalities in their own right. This means that the story of the plane and the story of the people who created the plane are inextricably intertwined. In many cases, the perseverance and heroism of these people rubbed off on the wire and metal and somehow became part of the machine itself.

If this seems too romanticized a view, then there is hardly any reason to know anything about the people who created these planes or the circumstances of their creation. Simply look up the numbers (the flight speed, the range, etc.) and leave it at that. But there is more to a classic than just the numbers; greatness consists of many less tangible qualities, and this book is an attempt to work out what those qualities are.

OPPOSITE: This souvenir program from the 1931 Schneider Trophy competition bears a stylized drawing of a Supermarine S.6, the forerunner of the first truly advanced fighter plane, the Supermarine Spitfire. In 1931, the S.6 won the Schneider Cup for the third consecutive year, retiring the trophy and bringing it permanently to England. **LEFT:** Charles Lindbergh posing in front of the *Spirit of St. Louis*, the Ryan NYP in which he made his historic solo flight across the Atlantic. Lindbergh's remarkable feat made him quite possibly the most famous person of the twentieth century. **BELOW:** Considered by many to be the best fighter plane of World War I, the Sopwith F-1 Camel was truly an extraordinary aircraft. By combining a powerful rotary engine with double-aileron wings, Sopwith was able to produce a biplane that could match the amazing maneuverability of a Fokker Dr-1 triplane without sacrificing speed and power.

Chapter 1
The Wright Flyer (U.S.)

As one looks at the history of flight, one is struck by two opposing (one might even say contradictory) thoughts. On the one hand, given all the flying things we see around us all the time—birds, insects, bats, even some fish—why did it take humankind so long to learn how to fly? On the other hand, given that a human being cannot fly like a bird—human musculature would have to be many times stronger and more efficient—how did human beings manage to learn to fly at all? Until the nineteenth century, the history of flight is the history of humanity's frustrating battle with this contradiction: emulating birds was clearly a dead end, but (it seemed only reasonable to believe) birds have got to have something to do with flying.

The breakthrough came in the early 1800s, when Sir George Cayley resolved this paradox. Yes, he determined, wings were useful components in the fashioning of a flying machine: the curve of the upper surface of the wing made the air move faster over the top of the wing than across its straight undersurface, and this created a pressure difference—a "lift"—that kept the wing aloft. But wings could only work if the machine were moving forward, and this was where human and bird parted company. While birds are light enough and have complex, highly evolved mechanisms in their wings to propel themselves forward, humans required a different propulsion system.

Cayley had worked as an engineer on windmills and had worked out some of the problems of keeping a rotating windmill anchored. He knew that a rotating propeller (called an "airscrew" in that era) would propel anything connected to it. In 1849 he built a model of an aircraft: a triplane with a boatlike undercarriage and a tail fin assembly. The craft may have had a propeller (if it did, it may have been powered by a large rubber band), and if we are to accept his granddaughter's account, a young boy, and perhaps even Cayley's adult coachman, actually flew in the craft in the summer of that year.

The cold desolation of the sand dunes at Kill Devil Hill in December 1903 mirrored the isolation of the Wright brothers as they pursued their dream of flight.

During the second half of the nineteenth century, inventors and gadgeteers on two continents tried to apply Cayley's concepts and build a working "aeroplane" using steam engines to power the propellers; some of them may even have succeeded in limited ways. For instance, two British industrialists, William Samuel Henson and John Stringfellow, designed a steam-driven aircraft they called the Aerial. Depictions of the plane flying over the Great Wall or the Pyramids, designed to attract investors, were utterly fanciful, but the craft's design was fundamentally sound and surprisingly similar to transport aircraft designs of nearly a century later. Hiram Maxim's mammoth machine, which he tested in England in the 1890s, was restrained from lifting off by guardrails Maxim himself installed. When test witnesses repeatedly (but respectfully, since Maxim was world famous for inventing the machine gun) pointed this out to him, the irrepressible Maxim scoffed and insisted he was not interested in lifting off, but only in proving that the engine was powerful enough.

The last two decades of the nineteenth century saw most experimenters turn their attention to the details of wing design. For this, gliding was the most convenient testing venue, and several experimenters gained worldwide fame as intrepid gliders. The most famous and most influential of these was Otto Lilienthal, a German engineer who, with his brother Gustav, pursued a carefully planned series of experiments

designed to measure the lift of different wing configurations and test different ways of controlling a glide. In the course of his more than two thousand glides, Lilienthal became an international celebrity. He was probably about to try adding an engine and propellers to one of his gliders when, in August 1896, his glider was tilted too far upward by a gust of wind, which caused it to stall and crash. Lilienthal's back was broken in the accident, and his death the next day made headlines the world over, including Dayton, Ohio, where two brothers had been following his exploits with growing interest and admiration.

Many excellent biographies have been written about Wilbur and Orville Wright, but the more thoroughly one searches, the greater becomes the enigma of the Wright brothers. They were two of five children, born four years apart (Wilbur in 1867 and Orville in 1871) to the family of a bishop of Dayton's United Brethren Church. Raised with midwestern Presbyterian values, they believed in the contemplative life and the virtue of hard work and perseverance. They were, however, remarkable in an eerie, almost otherworldly sense: the connection between them was so strong that each claimed to know what the other was thinking, almost before he thought it. Living with a kind of austere regimen that appeared to outsiders as almost robotic, they rarely showed any emotion.

They worked together in several enterprises that were not very successful, until they opened a bicycle shop in 1893 and began manufacturing bicycles of their own design. The country was then in the midst of a cycling craze, so they soon became financially independent—perhaps even rich, though their spartan lifestyle never permitted them an ostentatious display of wealth.

Soon after the reports of Lilienthal's death, the brothers began looking into the possibility of flight—and of devoting their time, energy, and resources to building an airplane. They corresponded with other experimenters in the field, including Octave Chanute, a retired midwestern railroad engineer who had pioneered the use of the Pratt truss—a bridge-building device that used taut cables and tightly tensioned beams to create greater strength and stability—in the construction of gliders. Chanute was generous with information and encouraged the Wrights, as did Samuel Pierpont Langley, Secretary of the Smithsonian Institution and a self-taught scientist who had been working on developing an airplane with support from the U.S. government.

LEFT: The fateful moment when humankind—in the person of Orville Wright—first flew, captured in one of the most remarkable photos in the history of technology. The time: 10:35 A.M. The date: December 17, 1903. The place: Kitty Hawk, North Carolina. The photographer: John T. Daniels, a local weatherman operating a camera set up for just this purpose by Wilbur Wright, seen running alongside the Flyer. **RIGHT:** The simple motor that made the Wright brothers' flight possible. The four horizontal cylinders were made of cast iron, but the rest of the engine was lightweight aluminum. The motor produced 12 horsepower, and it weighed only 160 pounds (72.5kg).

Many have speculated on the reason for the preponderance of brother teams in the early history of aviation. One author, alluding to the Wrights, suggested that flight was so difficult, it had to be done "by people with two heads and four hands."

With typical thoroughness, the brothers read everything they could get their hands on about flight and even consulted with the U.S. Weather Bureau about where the winds were most conducive to glider testing. The bureau recommended the dunes of Kill Devil Hill near Kitty Hawk, North Carolina, on the Atlantic coast, because it had the highest average measured winds on the East Coast. What the Wrights did not know, though they would learn soon enough, was that this high average was the result of long periods of gales and storms, followed by long periods of dead calm. In the end, it was the seclusion and the cushioning effect of the sand, and not the winds, that the Wrights appreciated most about Kitty Hawk. They first traveled from Dayton to the shore in October 1900, and returned in 1902 and again in 1903, to test their machines and devices.

The period from 1900 to the end of 1903 saw the Wrights embark on a development program that is as amazing for its painstaking patience as it is for its perseverance. With little guidance from the outside (only Chanute offered them advice and even visited them at Kitty Hawk), and with no way of knowing how close Langley and other rivals might be to inventing the airplane, they proceeded with a slow deliberation that must have tested even their steely resolve. They spent nearly a full year testing and measuring airfoil (wing) performance in a wind tunnel of their own design (decades ahead of its time, as it turned out) in the back of their bicycle shop.

To read Orville's account, *How We Invented the Airplane*, one might think the entire enterprise was "a day at the beach." In fact, the trip to

Kitty Hawk—by train from Dayton and then by wagon to the shore—was difficult, and the weather was usually unbearably cold. The brothers were not able to take their machines to North Carolina until they had finished the preliminary building and testing in Dayton in the summer months, which meant they would not set up camp at Kitty Hawk until September at the earliest. (Recall that their historic first flight took place in December, on one of the last days of the season when the weather would permit any thought of flying.)

Almost all the information they had read or received about the technicalities of flight turned out to be wrong, and the brothers had to test and measure everything anew in order to build an airplane that would perform as predicted. They conducted landmark experiments of propeller design as well as wing configuration, and constructed a gasoline engine that produced 12 horsepower while weighing only 160 pounds (72.5kg)—a feat that mechanics and engineers of the day would have said was impossible.

The fateful day was December 17, 1903, when, before five witnesses from the Kitty Hawk Weather Station, one of whom operated the tripod camera Wilbur had set up, Orville piloted the first aircraft capable of taking off, flying, maneuvering, and landing. The flight took all of twelve seconds, covered only 120 feet (36.5m), and rose only about fifteen feet (4.5m) off the ground. But there was no doubt about what the Wrights had accomplished, and (contrary to popular myth) the press reports nationwide acknowledged, albeit reservedly, the Wright brothers' achievement.

The full import of what the Wrights had accomplished did not become clear until 1908, during one of history's most delicious moments of silence. While Orville was wrangling with the U.S. Army over the sale of airplanes to them (after the army had been burned by the failure of Langley's machine), Wilbur traveled to France with one of his machines and demonstrated the Flyer at Le Mans during an aviation meet. During his two-minute flight, Wilbur darted about in circles, tight figure-eights, and dives, demonstrating such a command of the craft that the crowd of aviation enthusiasts below looked up dumbstruck. When he landed, the heretofore stone silent crowd, aware that they had just witnessed a miracle, erupted in pandemonium, and the Wrights (along with their sister, Katherine) became the toast of Europe and soon of the world.

What drove the Wrights? Biographers have pointed to their fascination with a toy helicopter their father gave them as children, or the kites they made and sold to their schoolmates; Wilbur referred to his involvement with flight as his "affliction"—meaning, probably, what would now be called an obsession. But the truth is that the Wrights came onto the aviation scene from out of nowhere, out of a clear blue sky. With the kind of heightened consciousness that was theirs alone, they set out to accomplish some-

The plane that the Wrights to sold the U.S. Army, shown here just prior to its test flight on June 29, 1909, carried two people at a top speed of 47 miles per hour (75.5kph). The Wrights would probably have preferred every ounce of weight to go into speed and maneuverability, without having to allow for bombs, armament, cameras, or electronics. This was one reason why the Wrights were eventually eclipsed by other designers.

thing truly extraordinary, and they did not for a moment allow such trifling things as physical hardship, mechanical frustration, faulty information, the elements, boredom, ridicule, or the disinterest of the rest of the world to deter them from their single-minded quest for flight.

The same stubborn determination that saw them through Kitty Hawk also kept them stubbornly devoted to features of the Flyer and subsequent models that others later showed to be clearly outdated and inferior. For years, the Wrights refused to put wheels on the undercarriage of their planes, and they never did adopt flaps and hinged control surfaces as the means of maneuvering instead of their "wing-warping" system. But the Flyer was studied, copied, and enhanced by aviators on both sides of the Atlantic, and it was still years before any aircraft could duplicate its performance in either agility or endurance. The enterprise of human flight had taken a giant leap into the air—on the shoulders of two solemn-looking brothers from Ohio and the wings of their spindly aircraft, the Flyer. As one looks at the Flyer (renamed the Kitty Hawk) hanging in the Smithsonian, one can sense its elegant economy, like an utterance out of Orville's mouth. Yet from its terse lines roared forth a century of aviation history.

Chapter 2
The Blériot XI (France)

I n the years following Kitty Hawk, an intense international competition arose between aircraft manufacturers in France and the United States. The French had been the first to fly in a balloon and they believed that flying was the special province of France; for all the acclaim they poured on the Wrights, French aircraft manufacturers were determined to regain preeminence in aviation. The opportunity to take the lead arose in 1909. In the United States, the Wright brothers were embroiled in a bitter and distracting patent dispute with Glenn Curtiss, a self-taught airplane designer whose genius for aeronautical engineering was matched only by his talent for throwing legal obstacles in the Wrights' path. The British, satisfied that the theoretical underpinnings of flight had been established by the Englishman Cayley, and still hurting from the failure of the Henson and Stringfellow enterprise (the inventors had been subjected to intense public ridicule for their ham-fisted attempts to raise money to build their Aerial), stepped aside and embraced the Wright brothers' design. In an effort to inspire further progress in British aviation, the London *Daily Mail* offered a £1,000 prize to the first man to fly across the English Channel in daylight.

While the Wrights focused their attention on selling airplanes to governments and the military (the only customers who could afford the $200,000 price tag they put on their invention), the Voisin brothers, Charles and Gabriel, were doing a thriving business from their factory outside Paris, manufacturing airplanes for flying enthusiasts all over Europe. Unlike the Wrights, the Voisins built planes to the specifications of their customers, most of whom had no grasp of the principles of aerodynamics or any idea how to design an airplane that would actually fly. Many of the aircraft they produced crashed, which turned airplanes into perishable products the Voisins were happy to replenish. The beneficiaries of all this experimenting were the Voisins themselves, who learned a great deal about what would not fly from their hapless customers. By the time they were approached by their biggest customer,

Louis Blériot in the cockpit of the Type XI airplane in which he made his historic flight. Blériot is probably the most tenacious, if not the most talented, of the early pioneers of aviation.

Louis Blériot, they had learned a great deal, and they could probably have manufactured an aircraft for him that would fly well enough to claim the *Daily Mail* prize.

Blériot, however, was simply not the kind of man to avail himself of someone else's knowledge. He was a tall and portly man, given to manic bursts of enthusiasm and quixotic schemes. He had made a fortune manufacturing accessories for automobiles, hitting it big with acetylene head lamps and then squandering all of it pursuing aviation. His approach contrasted markedly to the Wrights: he rarely conducted tests or took measurements, and was giving the Voisins new designs even before he had tried (and crashed) the old ones. Had Blériot not

already made his mark in automobiles, he would have become famous (or notorious) for being the man who had crashed planes most often. As new and ever stranger design elements came from Blériot's fertile imagination, Gabriel tried to set him straight (without alienating a paying customer). By the time Blériot was ready to attempt a Channel crossing, he was using borrowed money and was up to his eleventh model, aptly known as the Blériot XI.

The design of the Blériot XI represented a radical departure from the design approach of the Wrights. The Flyer was designed to be inherently unstable in order to allow maximum maneuverability. Taking a lesson from Lilienthal's career, the Wrights believed an aircraft should be completely controlled by the pilot, even in straight, level flight. Without the constant working of the wings, the elevators, and the rudder, a Flyer would go into a spin and crash to earth; in the hands of a capable pilot, the aircraft could safely follow virtually any path in the air for as long as the fuel lasted.

The Europeans, on the other hand, believed the design goal was to produce an aircraft that was inherently stable—an airplane that would practically fly itself. This difference in approach was quickly translated into design differences: it was soon apparent that "tractor" propulsion (propellers on the front end of the craft pulling the rest of the plane behind) was more conducive to stability than "pusher" propulsion (the propeller in the rear pushing the aircraft). The Flyer was a pusher-propelled aircraft (the Wrights did use both configurations), but Europeans nearly always used tractor-propelled design.

Soon a design model emerged that used a single-wing (monoplane) instead of a double-wing (biplane) design, placing the elevator and rud-

46891

ABOVE: This front view of the Blériot XI reveals a simple but sturdy construction, and the name of the engine's manufacturer, Anzani, is clearly emblazoned on the motor. **LEFT:** Takeoff was always an adventure in the early planes. After starting the engine, a crewman ran around to the back to help others hold the plane back until enough thrust was generated by the propeller, at which time the crew would let go and the plane would lunge forward.

der in the rear far back from the wing (on the Flyer, these control surfaces were close to the wing and in need of constant pilot manipulation), seating the pilot behind the wings (instead of on the lower wing, as in the Flyer), and moving the aircraft's center of gravity off the wings and between its airfoil's control surfaces. In this configuration, a plane could fly without active control by the pilot.

The Blériot XI was not yet this stable, but it and the other European entry into the Channel-crossing contest, the Antoinette VII, piloted by celebrated British aviator Hubert Latham, were headed in that direction. The third entrant in the contest was a Wright biplane built by Charles de Lambert, the French licensee for the Wright patents. De Lambert was first to attempt the crossing, but when his aircraft was damaged in a warm-up flight, he decided not to risk losing his craft (which was worth more than the prize).

Latham already held endurance and distance records and was famous throughout Europe. His plane, the Antoinette VII, had been the design of Leon Levavasseur, an engineer who had built the most efficient and reliable engine up to that time, though the design was a classic Voisin product. The debonair Latham probably thought the race was won when de Lambert withdrew, as Blériot, with his eccentric reputation and his ramshackle crew and craft, appeared to present little in the way of a serious challenge. On July 19, 1909, Latham took off from his base in Calais, but crashed into the sea seven miles (11km) out. The ship that came to rescue him found the dapper aviator sitting calmly on the floating wing of his downed aircraft, smoking a cigarette in his well-known cigarette holder. The plane was towed back and repaired, and Latham went back to the Grand Hotel to prepare for another try (which entailed the imbibing of much champagne).

Blériot had meanwhile grappled with the problem of outfitting his aircraft with an engine powerful and reliable enough to take him across the Channel. He settled on an engine built by an irascible Italian bicycle racer, Alessandro Anzani. The Anzani engine was sturdy, light, and simple, putting out a meager 25 horsepower. But the Blériot XI was very light and was equipped with an improved Chauvier propeller, and the engine was easily powerful enough to get the plane across...if it remained cool enough. (Subsequent tests with the Anzani showed that a properly constructed model could not run the thirty-seven minutes it took Blériot to cross the Channel.) Two lucky breaks made the flight

RIGHT, TOP: The Blériot XI makes landfall near Dover. RIGHT, BOTTOM: In 1909 European aircraft such as the Blériot XI had evolved into a very different type of design from the Wrights', and became one that would influence future aeronautic designers much more than the ten more successful Wright planes.

possible: a leaky oil line that sprayed hot oil out of the engine (and onto Blériot's leg, bandaged because of a crash just days earlier), lowering the engine temperature, and a sudden rain shower that further cooled the exposed engine.

In the early morning hours of July 25, 1909, after several days of stormy weather, Blériot saw (or thought he saw) a brief clearing and took off. Levavasseur, who had spent the night looking anxiously at the sky, aware that Blériot was ready to make a desperate try at the prize, had urged Latham to be ready, telling him that he might be able to take off the next morning. Latham scoffed, lit another cigarette, called for room service, and slept the night away. Levavasseur was awakened at 4:30 A.M. by cries that indicated Blériot had taken off, and rushed to the window just in time to catch a glimpse of the Blériot XI disappearing into the Channel mist. Latham was dismayed to learn that Blériot had taken off and, with a typically British sense of gamesmanship, tried to convince Levavasseur to let him take off after Blériot. By that point, however, the skies had darkened again, and the engineer (who was, no doubt, feeling rather angry with his pilot at this point) decided not to put the plane in the air. A crestfallen Latham sent a telegram to Dover congratulating Blériot in case he should succeed.

Several times during Blériot's brief flight there was a good chance he would crash either into the sea or into the cliffs of Dover; without any navigational equipment aboard (which he had never troubled to carry or even learn how to use) it was sheer luck that

he found the crack in the cliff wall and landed (or crash-landed) in the field near Dover Castle where a crowd was waiting. The photos of Blériot emerging from his crashed airplane show a haggard man, the pain from his scalded leg clear on his face.

The success meant a new windfall for Blériot (which he eventually squandered again), as orders for Blériot planes came pouring in. In addition to the stable design, Blériot had pioneered the control system that remained standard on airplanes for years: a foot control for the rear rudder, a central "joystick" control for both the elevator and the wing-warping (later for the ailerons), and a second hand lever for the throttle. The Blériot planes, outfitted with the much sounder French Gnome rotary engines in place of the Anzani (the unreliability of which made Blériot's feat seem even more miraculous), became standard all over Europe. It was not long before military planners began to consider the possible military applications of airplanes, particularly for an attack against the British Isles, previously thought to be impregnable.

Hubert Latham did finally make an attempt to cross the Channel three days after Blériot, but his plane crashed into the sea just a few hundred yards away from the coast of Dover. Latham was hurt badly in the crash, and retired from flying in order to pursue his next favorite pastime: big-game hunting. Within two years he was dead, killed by a charging buffalo while he was on safari in Africa. Like many aircraft manufacturers of the time (including Blériot), Levavasseur and de Lambert wound up in bankruptcy court.

LEFT, TOP: Hubert Latham, known throughout Europe as a man of great style and flying prowess, was the odds-on favorite to win the Daily Mail prize. LEFT, BOTTOM: A sailor aboard the French torpedo boat *Harpon* prods the ditched Antoinette VII looking for a lift point.

Chapter 3
The Fokker D-VII (Germany)

No Hollywood screenwriter could ever have dreamed up (or would ever have dared to) a life or a character like Anthony Fokker. Born in Java in 1891, the son of wealthy Dutch coffee plantation owners, young Tony was a carefree boy who spent his days playing on the beach with the children of the plantation workers. In 1897, the family returned to Holland for Anthony's schooling, but by then the free-spirited boy was ill-suited to the formal rigors of the Dutch classroom.

Early on, Tony showed an uncanny ability for mechanical invention: he devised a four-pointed pen so that he could write the lines he was given as punishment for misbehavior in a quarter of the time. He converted the attic into his own private workshop and built an elaborate electric train set. (His parents were probably less than thrilled at his connecting the electric wire to the knob of the attic door in order to safeguard his privacy.) The young Tony Fokker clearly showed all the qualities of the man he would become: unbridled exuberance, self-assurance, arrogance, cockiness, and selfishness. He was to be a charming, cunning, talented rogue.

Predictably, Fokker left school and announced that, though just barely a teenager, he was going to develop an automobile tire that would not require air (and thus would never go flat). Herman Fokker, Tony's father, supported his son's ambition and, when a patent suit ensued, paid dearly for the lawyers who followed the case to its end—a bitter end, as it turned out, since the court upheld another inventor's earlier patent. At one point during this phase of Fokker's career, he and his father attended an automobile show in Brussels, where a plane flown by Hubert Latham was on exhibit. Herman turned to his son and said angrily that, no matter what, he would never buy his son an airplane. In later years, Tony claimed that the thought had never occurred to him until his father mentioned it. That night, the young inventor was in the attic, tinkering with wooden models and turning his prodigious mind to the problems of aircraft design.

ABOVE: After getting rich by supplying the German military with his airplanes, Tony Fokker managed to slip back to his native Holland at the end of World War I with his fortune intact, and was back in business within a few months. **OPPOSITE:** The D-VII was one of the greatest aircraft of World War I. This restored D-VII was flown by German ace Willie Gabriel. It's still flown in exhibitions.

The Eindecker ("single-wing") E-III represented a simple extension of the French Voisin design (note the reliance on bracing wires) with a powerful Le Rhone engine. The cowling over the engine was designed to protect the engine and the timing mechanism of the gun, and to protect the pilot and ground crew from the rotating engine. Fokker did not realize that the cowling also vastly reduced engine drag, and it did not appear on later models.

ations to barnstormers, and earning a reputation as a man as agile with the truth as he was in a plane. He carried on a voluminous correspondence with his father, and the theme of these letters ran along the same lines year after year: artful pleas for more money and impassioned promises to repay (or were the pleas impassioned and the promises artful?) Herman, by all accounts as cantankerous as an old man as he had been as a young man, wrote angry replies and swore he would disown his son—but he always included money and, in all, supported Tony to the tune of some 200,000 marks. He later admitted that he did this because he hadn't been much of a student in school himself and knew that a young man's dreams often needed an older man's financing. During the war, when Fokker became wealthy, he repaid his father everything he had gotten from him, with interest.

What exactly Tony Fokker discovered about aerodynamics up in his attic is unclear, since he was not above exaggerating his accomplishments or presenting the work of others as his own. He claimed to have discovered the aerodynamic advantages of the swept-back wing and of dihedral design. (Dihedral means the wing slopes upward as it leaves the fuselage; anhedral design means the wing slopes downward.) Whether or not he made these discoveries independently, Fokker-built planes were the first to successfully apply these concepts.

When the tire lawsuit had run its course, Tony's parents frantically enrolled him in a German engineering school. Tony convinced his father to allow him to transfer to another engineering school just twenty miles (32km) away, neglecting to mention that it was a school of aeronautical engineering. When Herman found out, he threatened to cut off funds, but Tony convinced him to attend a ceremony in which his instructor would pilot a plane the school had built on its maiden flight. In a life filled with schemes, bluffs, hype, and promotion, Tony Fokker's talents were probably never so severely tested as when he had to convince his father to let him remain at the school after the ceremony ended with the plane crashing, killing the instructor.

In the decade prior to World War I, Fokker pursued an active life on the fringes of aviation, building and flying planes, selling his cre-

When war broke out in August 1914, Fokker's fortunes turned; within hours, German officers who had treated him like an annoying gnat just days earlier were bidding wildly for everything in his shop. The war was expected to last only a few months, and the German army needed aircraft for battlefield reconnaissance. Two unexpected things happened: the war was not over in two months, and in the spring of 1915, German airplanes began to disappear mysteriously during their missions. In April, a French Morane-Saulnier monoplane was forced to land behind German lines when its engine failed, and the Germans' worst fear was confirmed: strapped to the top of the fuselage was a Lewis gun, and on the propeller blades were large plates designed to deflect the bullets that did not pass between the propeller blades.

The job of duplicating the Morane-Saulnier system was given to Fokker, who had never before handled a gun but was convinced that there had to be a better way. He envisioned a mechanical synchronizing gear between the gun and the propeller that would not allow the gun to fire when the blade was directly in front of the barrel. Fokker's account of the development of his mechanism has almost religious overtones, and ignores the facts that both sides had been working on just such a device since before the war and, indeed, that several engineers were close to perfecting it anyway when he burst on the scene.

Fokker may well have concocted the story to hide the fact that he had, at one point, offered to develop a similar mechanism for the British earlier in the war, but had been turned away. Fokker had to demonstrate his device himself. He seems to have taken a good deal of pleasure in diving toward the assembled officers and sending them running frantically for cover.

Fokker's combination of the interrupter timing mechanism with his aircraft—a design embarrassingly close to the captured Morane-Saulnier—and the Oberursel engine (a dead ringer for the French Gnome) resulted in Fokker's first great World War I fighter, the Fokker E-I Eindecker. The E-I and its descendants, the E-II and E-III, controlled the skies above Europe in what became known to the French and British as the Fokker Scourge.

If Tony Fokker's career had followed the path of other aviation pioneers, this would have been its culmination, and after making his fortune, and perhaps even keeping it, he would have succumbed to the pressures of larger and better-managed companies that copied his designs (just as he had helped himself to the work of others). However, this did not happen. First, he stayed in close contact with the pilots who flew his planes, providing them with luxuriant surroundings and

RIGHT: The DrI triplane had short wings that presented poor targets to ground artillery and enemy aircraft. Note also how the bracing wires have been replaced with a few metal braces, making a direct hit on the fuselage, a near-impossible shot, the only way to bring down the aircraft.

LEFT: Once Tony Fokker had a chance to show the German High command what his D-VII could do with a Mercedes engine, his career was assured. For the remainder of the war, he had the pleasure of seeing his competitors forced to produce his plane under contract.

The fighter pilots of World War I were, for the most part, individualistic and aristocratic daredevils. The common soldiers in the trenches soon came to resent the praise and adulation that was heaped on dashing aces such as von Richtofen, whose exploits, in the end, had little or no effect on the outcome of the war.

RIGHT, BOTTOM: The D-VII cockpit had only the bare essentials as far as flight controls were concerned. The dual mounted machine guns had an interrupter mechaninism to keep the bullets from shooting off the propeller.

listening carefully to their criticisms and observations. Secondly, he studied every plane that was downed by the Germans and adapted anything of use that was coming out of the Allied factories. Finally, he spent all his time at the front, talking to the mechanics, pilots, gunners, and anyone who might have a constructive suggestion. He lived so simple and driven an existence that he was known as *der Alter*—"the old man"—to his workers and the townspeople, though he was still in his early twenties.

Out of this approach came two other Fokker designs, each a masterpiece and each important to the conduct of the war. First came the triplanes, chief among them the Fokker Dr-1, the plane made famous by Manfred von Richthofen, the Red Baron. The Dr-1 had three wings (actually four, since the strut between the wheels was also an airfoil that could be controlled), and delicately balanced ailerons that allowed the plane, in von Richthofen's words, "to climb like a monkey and maneuver like the devil." The Dr-1's maneuverability masked the fact that it was not a

fast plane, and it proved too difficult to fly for any but the most gifted pilots. But in the hands of such a pilot, the Dr-1 was a dangerous adversary. Only 320 Dr-1s were ever produced (partly because its special "braceless" metal construction made it expensive to manufacture), and the plane was outperformed by its more versatile ancestor, the Sopwith Camel. But the legacy of the Red Baron, and the special ethos of the fighter pilot, date to this era and this plane.

Fokker's greatest achievement was the D-VII, a plane that came into existence as the result of a gamble only he would attempt. He knew that the Albatross Company's lock on the use of the Mercedes engine was eventually going to put his company out of business, yet the giant Albatross was still no match for him. Fokker tried every conventional means of getting permission to use the Mercedes engine, and a few means only he could dream up, but to no avail. So he appealed to von Richthofen (who, after all, had an interest in having the best possible planes at his disposal) to force the government into conducting a competition to see who could produce the best plane. In order to best be able to judge the performance of the plane, von Richthofen insisted, over the outraged objections of the Albatross executives, that Mercedes engines be used and made available to all the contestants. Fokker at last had his hands on the engine he wanted.

The trials were held on January 18, 1918. The other companies, eager to court the pilots, threw lavish parties during the days leading up to the trial, with the result that some of their pilots were so hungover they could barely fly. Fokker had come with eight different designs, and he dealt with von Richthofen personally and on a strictly professional level. When the Baron selected one of Fokker's designs to test, a biplane based on Reinhold Platz's design of the Dr-1, rumors ran through the camp that the Baron had selected Fokker. But the test flight did not go well. Fokker had lengthened the wing span to accommodate the greater power of the Mercedes engine, but without changing the fuselage or the "empennage" (the tail assembly) of the aircraft. Fokker mumbled something about a problem with the landing gear and took the plane into his hangar for the night. There, he and his mechanics worked feverishly for three days straight, cutting the fuselage and inserting a two-foot (61cm) section that lengthened the fuselage and increased the fin. The result was the Fokker D-VII, a plane that was decades ahead of its time; indeed, it remained in service in some air forces into the 1930s.

The combination of speed and agility exhibited by the D-VII was unequaled in any previous plane, and in some ways it remains unequaled to this day. The D-VII could perform maneuvers that would be beyond the capability of other aircraft for decades. The D-VII was able to change direction without banking, merely by working the rudder, which radically cut down the time and space required for a turn; it could also glide at an angle—even upside down—when other planes would stall. This maneuver, called "hanging on its propeller," gives the viewer the impression that the plane is not flying at all, but is being carried across the sky by a giant invisible hand.

After von Richthofen put the D-VII through its paces, General von Hoeppner, head of the German air force, took Fokker aside and asked, "How many of these planes could you build at once, Herr Fokker?" Fokker said he could not produce many because his factories were cluttered with Albatross and AEG models he had been ordered to build. Von Hoeppner told him he would no longer have to build anything but the D-VII; in fact, Albatross and AEG would be forced to build D-VIIs to supplement the Fokker factory output, and pay Fokker a royalty for each plane. Fokker had the delicious pleasure of being able to pass judgment on how well his rivals were producing his plane. He charged the German government 10 million marks for four hundred planes, a staggering price, but the performance of the D-VII in the theater of battle justified the expenditure, even if air power did not in the end play a decisive role in determining the outcome of the war. The D-VII was the only aircraft specifically identified by the Armistice agreement as booty for the Allies.

By the war's end, Fokker had amassed a large fortune and had taken nearly all of it out of Germany, back to his native Holland, along with four hundred Mercedes engines, 220 complete D-VII airframes, and 120 fully armed and appointed D-VIIs, smuggled out of Germany by train. His German patron had lost the war, but Fokker was back in business within a few months, having never lost a beat. To Tony Fokker's many admirers and critics, this came as no surprise.

The rebuilt D-VII shown here is still flown at exhibitions. It is difficult to imagine how unnerving Allied fighter pilots found the D-VII's ability to turn without banking, or to fly upside down as easily, it seemed, as right side up.

Chapter 4
The Spad 13 (France)

The fighter planes—even the great ones—used on both sides in World War I were extensions of designs and concepts developed by experimenters and manufacturers before the war. The Fokker planes were derived from earlier Morane-Saulnier models; the French Nieuport and Britain's Sopwith Scout were brilliant developments of prewar designs. But the Spad series of planes, the most famous of which was the Spad 13, represented a new phase in aircraft development, one that was to be studied and emulated for decades—this in spite of the fact that in face-to-face confrontations in the skies, the Spad planes were outperformed by several other fighters during World War I.

The Spad was produced by the Société pour Aviation et ses Derivés, a company that grew out of a company founded by French silk magnate Armand Deperdussin, an amateur aviation enthusiast. Deperdussin recruited aircraft designer Louis Bechereau, one of the great airplane designers in the history of aviation. In 1913, Deperdussin racers captured both the Gordon Bennett and the Schneider trophies, and some observers believed the lead that France enjoyed in aviation as a result of Deperdussin was enough to dissuade Germany from going to war. In 1914, however, a stock manipulation scandal led to the dismissal of Deperdussin. The reorganization of the company was placed in the hands of (of all people) national hero and rival manufacturer Louis Blériot. Of Blériot's many ups and downs, his stewardship of the Deperdussin organization was among his successes. He kept intact the company elements vital to the development of new aircraft technology, especially Bechereau; he made sure there would be adequate funding for a development program; and the new name he gave the company, Société pour les Appareils Deperdussin, retained the SPAD acronym.

Blériot's plan worked, and SPAD was producing important aircraft for the French army within months. The most lasting contribution

Lieutenant Eddie Rickenbacker of the famed 94th Aero Pursuit "Hat-in-the-Ring" Squadron, posing in front of his Spad 13 aircraft. Note the automotive-style radiator grill behind the propeller. Though the fuselage is much more developed than earlier aircraft, the wings still rely on wire bracing, and the landing gear is simpler than that on earlier planes.

made by SPAD, however, was the development of the construction techniques Bechereau had pioneered in the Deperdussin Monocoque racer. The problem Bechereau had set out to solve was how to build a plane strong enough to hold a powerful stationary engine, yet light enough to provide high speed and performance. Earlier, designers were able to get more power per pound from rotary engines, in which the cylinders rotated around a stationary piston. As a rotary engine became larger, the gyroscopic effect of the rotating engine bloc became significant, and airplanes equipped with these engines became unmanageable. Once planes reached a weight greater than eighteen hundred pounds (817kg), rotary engines had to be replaced with the heavier stationary engines. (After the war, when planes became much heavier, their weight was enough to overcome these gyroscopic effects, and efficient rotary engines made a comeback.)

Bechereau faced two challenges: finding a powerful and efficient engine, and putting it into a light but strong airframe. For the engine, Bechereau had heard about an advanced V-8 engine developed by a Swiss engineer, Mark Birkigt, working in Spain for the Hispano-Suiza automobile company. The company had a factory in France, from which Bechereau obtained a test model. The engine amazed the French engineer, and he was determined to house it in as strong and as light an airframe as he could build.

For this Bechereau did not have far to look. Just before the war, he had experimented with a new kind of construction he called mono-

coque, or "single shell." Previously, the frames of airplanes were constructed out of struts assembled like the framework of a building, over which the skin—usually canvas—was stretched. The limitations of this design were clear: the canvas could not bear any of the weight of the plane; it was prone to tear away from (or be shot off) the frame; and, as planes became larger, the framework became much heavier. If the skin could be made of a metal or solid material, it might be able to support some of the structure, and the result would be a lighter and more rigid aircraft. The Deperdussin monocoque was made of wood and did not require lightening, but it demonstrated the technique and the stability

RIGHT, TOP: The Deperdussin Monocoque Racer, designed by Louis Bechereau, was unveiled in 1912. It was the first to use monocoque construction of the fuselage, though the fuselage was made of wood and the wings were still braced by wire and covered with doped canvas.

RIGHT, BOTTOM: The fact that a light plane like the Duperdussin Racer could support a heavy, powerful engine, and with it win the 1912 Gordon Bennett Trophy, changed aircraft construction overnight.

of the design. Now, with the heavier Hispano-Suiza engine, mono-coque construction was going to become a necessity.

The result was the Spad 7, a streamlined aircraft with thin venetian blind wings and a front grill that curiously (but understandably) resembled the front of an automobile. It quickly became the favorite of the French aces, and nearly all the great French fliers—such as René Fonck and Georges Guynemer—flew Spad 7s. By the time American fliers of the Lafayette Escadrille entered the war, the Spad 7s were being outclassed by German fighter planes, and the series was upgraded until Bechereau produced the Spad 13, the plane flown to glory by Eddie Rickenbacker and the famed 94th Aero Pursuit "Hat-in-the-Ring" Squadron.

The Spad 13 was a deceptive design, insofar as it outwardly appeared to be a throwback to earlier designs. It used tension wires like the old prewar biplanes, the streamlined fuselage made it appear fragile, and takeoffs and landings were always bumpy affairs. But in combat, it proved durable, fast (30 percent faster than its adversaries), and highly

The water-tight hull created by the monocoque fuselage encouraged adaptation of the Spad aircraft as a pontoon-equipped sea-plane. Water would also provide a safer and softer landing surface until better landing gear could be developed.

maneuverable. It was also much easier to fly than the German planes, which meant that many more pilots could be trained and placed in it. By the end of the war, some eight thousand Spad 13s had seen service, overwhelming the German forces by their sheer numbers.

The fighters of World War I were not an important strategic part of the war because of the absence of a significant bomber component. Both sides were busy developing such a program, and had the war continued even a few more months, significant bombing campaigns would almost certainly have been launched, which would have required fighter protection. As it was, the fighters fought each other rather pointlessly for dominance of the sky, which was of only sporting interest to the troops below. The British even discouraged the lionization of aces because of the demoralizing effect on ground troops. But the prospect of airpower possibly playing a role in that (or a future) war propelled development of aviation technology during the war years. The mono-coque design was one major result, and virtually no plane built after the war was without this feature.

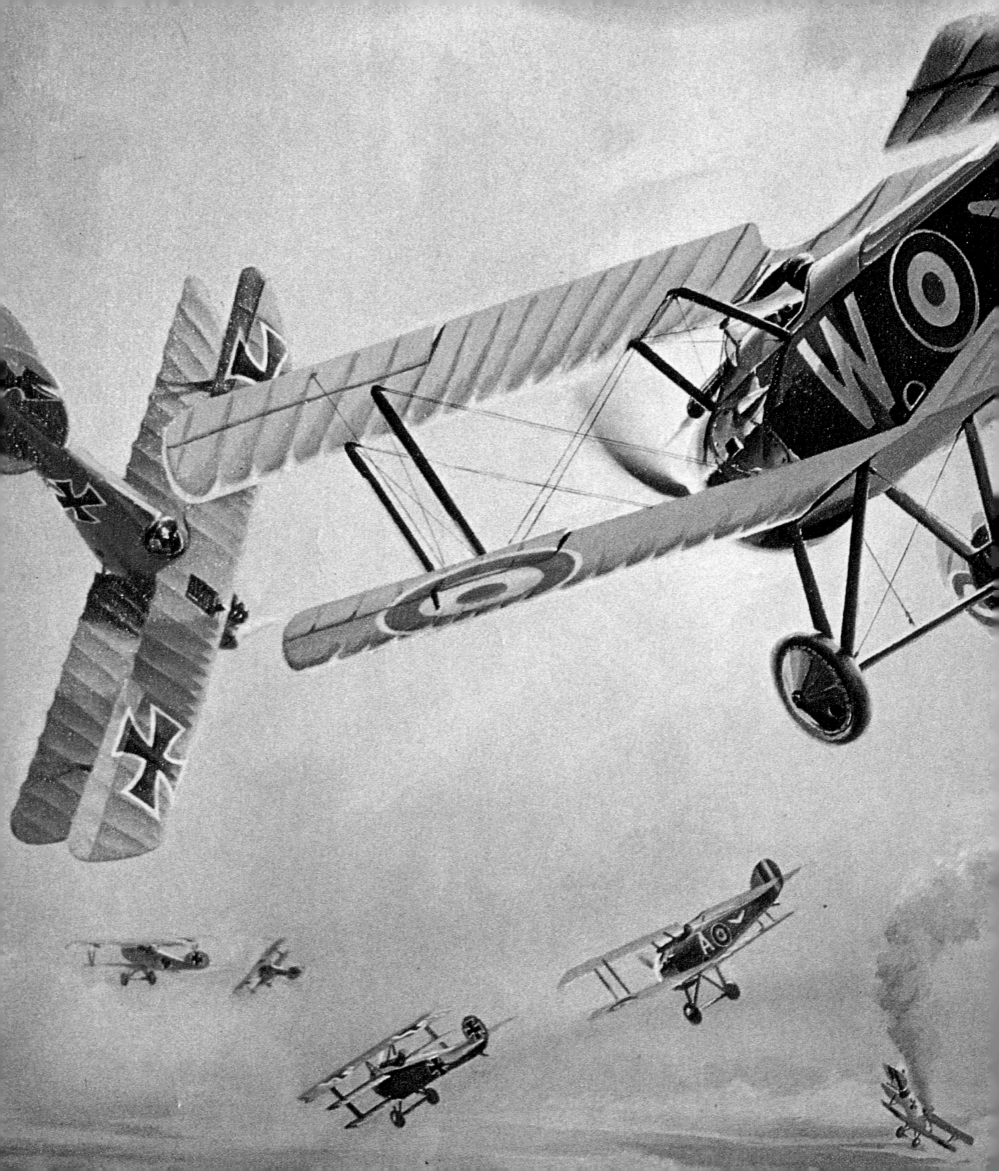

Chapter 5
The Sopwith Camel (U.K.)

ABOVE: The young patrician "Tom" Sopwith chanced upon two French fliers at the end of a record-setting flight—a happenstance that changed the course of aviation history.

OPPOSITE: An Australian mural commemorating the fighter aces of World War I, featuring the Sopwith Camel.

When T.O.M. (Thomas Octave Murdoch) Sopwith docked his yacht at Dover Harbor in the summer of 1910, the young British aristocrat was looking forward to little more than a gin and tonic and a leisurely life filled with yacht races and cotillions. The town was abuzz, however, with excitement over the news that a plane making the first successful flight across the English Channel with a passenger on board had landed. Sopwith followed the crowd to the landing site and was amazed to see the men who had accomplished the history-making feat: the diminutive John B. Moisant and his burly auto mechanic. This couldn't be all that difficult, he thought.

That was Sopwith's introduction to the world of aviation, and it turned out to be a fateful moment for flight as well as for England. Within three months, Sopwith had flown in a plane, purchased a Farman of his own, learned to pilot it, and received Aviator's Certificate Number 31 from the Royal Aero Club. By the end of the year, Sopwith had won the Baron de Forest Cup for the longest flight from England to the European continent by an all-English crew. He flew 169 miles (272km) from Eastchurch to Thirimont, France, receiving the cup and pocketing the £4,000 cash prize, all within six months of first setting eyes on a plane. More importantly, however, Sopwith teamed up with an old friend, Harry Hawker (who had already been experimenting in aviation for a few years), to create the Sopwith Aviation Company. (Guess whose family supplied the seed money.)

Sopwith spent the next summer in the United States, attending aerial meets and soaking up the influences of American aeronautical designs. This can be seen in the design of the Sopwith Bat Boat, which incorporates many design elements of the Curtiss NC boat planes. In the early days of flight, many designers borrowed freely from one another since there were few opportunities to test most innovations or develop them methodically, and there was also no agency that could be relied on to verify the claims of inventors in this field.

LEFT: The Sopwith Pup was an extremely light plane—only eight hundred pounds (363kg) without fuel, pilot, or armament—that behaved surprisingly well at high altitudes. This made it perfect for attacking from above, making it the British plane that the Red Baron most feared.

BELOW: This Sopwith F-1 Camel bears the markings of England's Squadron No. 43.

Sopwith's travels and his mechanical approach to solving problems gave him a great deal of valuable experience on which to base his designs. He had also participated in—and won—the Schneider Cup race of 1914 with a Tabloid aircraft, powered by a 100-hp Gnome engine. The double-pontoon flotation system it used was put together the day of the race.

When war broke out in 1914, Sopwith was the foremost British airplane manufacturer, in the business by then for all of four years. The Germans were generally advanced over the British and the French in the air, but Sopwith's aircraft were so well designed that they eventually made up for deficiencies in manufacturing and outclassed their adversaries. Sopwith planes were particularly adept at integrating the mechanisms of gun-synchronizing gear and the Scarf Ring rotating machine-gun mount for rear-cockpit machine gunners.

Sopwith produced three series of planes during the war that became the foundation of the British air force. The first was the Type 9700, called the "One-and-a-Half Strutter," or just the "One-and-a-

Half," after the W-shaped struts that connected the upper and the lower wings. The One-and-a-Half combined features Sopwith had developed in the Schneider Cup competition, such as the dive break and the tilted tail assembly, with the Vickers and the Lewis machine guns—the best of their day—in order to match the planes with which the Germans had taken control of the sky.

Sopwith then designed a plane that was not just a cobbled-together assembly of previously developed components, but one in which all the elements were part of a unified and consistent design from the outset. The result was the Pup, a plane of incredible agility, weighing only eight hundred pounds (363kg) (without fuel, armament, or pilot) and powered by a scant 80-hp Le Rhone rotary engine.

Ever eager to try new configurations, Sopwith then went on to develop the Triplane (or "Tripe"), the plane used by the Canadian Black Flight squadron. The Sopwith Triplane became the model for the Fokker triplane flown by the Red Baron, Manfred von Richthofen; as the war progressed, air battles were increasingly fought by both sides in planes that were, in reality, the brainchild of one builder: Sopwith. Those battles would have been fought to a draw had Sopwith not had a better idea.

The idea behind the Triplane had been to give the plane more maneuverability by giving it more airfoil surfaces. This created more drag (air resistance), which cut down speed, but the agility of the plane could more than make up for that in battle. What if, Sopwith wondered, one could obtain such agility without sacrificing speed—say, by using only two wings with a more powerful engine and with double ailerons on each wing? After some experimenting, Sopwith and Hawker found that the only way to get the agility they wanted was to cram as much of the weight as possible in a small area between the wings. This would give the plane very little rotational inertia, and flight would be completely controlled by the surfaces of the wing.

The strongest engine they could find that would fit was the Clerget rotary engine, capable of producing 180 horsepower, and even then the fuselage had to be enlarged and given a hump to make the engine fit. This gave the aircraft its name: the Camel. The use of a rotary engine was a double-edged sword: the plane's rotational moment was so short that the rotating engine acted like a gyroscope, giving the plane a downward torque in a right turn and an upward torque in a left. The pilots could use this extra push to their advantage (for other, more balanced, aircraft, this torque effect was negligible); the fact that a Sopwith Camel favored a right-turn dive was among the most closely guarded secrets of the war.

Once the Camels flew—over five thousand were produced—the aerial war was all but over, and Britain ruled the skies. The Camel was considered the best fighter of the war, even though the design philosophy that created it was not one that could be extended very far. The Camel's agility made it a very difficult airplane to master, and it is likely that most of the pilots lost while flying Sopwith Camels were brought down not by enemy fire, but by the planes' flying characteristics and the pilots' own inexperience.

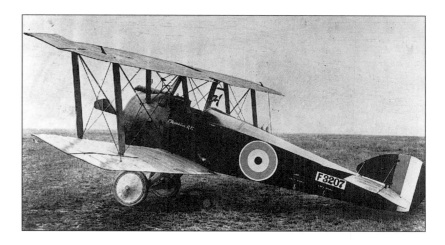

ABOVE: The Sopwith Camel, so named for the hump up front that contained the engine. LEFT: The Sopwith Triplane, advanced in design but not in construction; note the wire bracing, virtually absent from the Fokker version of the same plane. With the help of Harry Hawker, Sopwith was able to develop aircraft with better and better performance parameters, while other builders rarely explored new directions in design. Sopwith planes like the Snipe and the Dove soon took control of the European skies.

Chapter 6
The Sikorsky Ilya-Mourometz (U.S.S.R.)

The Russian Revolution of 1917 had its effect on the history of Russian aviation in two ways. The Soviet leadership waged a confused propaganda campaign regarding the work of Alexander Mozhaisky, claiming he had flown in 1884, nineteen years before the Wright brothers. Communist support of the Mozhaisky claim was halfhearted, because the entire enterprise of aviation before the revolution had been dominated by aristocrats and czarists. The revolution also turned most of the foremost designers, builders, and pilots—those who had not been executed—into refugees.

Among those executed was General Mikhail Shidlovsky, head of the Russo-Baltic Railcar Factory, the center for aviation manufacturing in czarist Russia. One of Shidlovsky's protégés, a brilliant Russian designer from Moscow enthralled with aviation since boyhood, managed to escape by hiding in a tramp steamer out of Murmansk. In March 1919, he disembarked in New York, and began his second (and by no means his last) illustrious career in aviation. His name was Igor Sikorsky, and he had already built an entire air force for Russia by the time he was thirty years old.

Sikorsky joined Shidlovsky's group in 1912 when he won a contest with a home-built aircraft that flew at seventy miles per hour (112.5 kph). With a firm tradition of aeronautical research behind them (as found in the work of Nikolai Zhukovsky, "the father of Russian aviation"), Shidlovsky gave Sikorsky a free hand and almost limitless funds to develop aircraft and experiment.

The first plane Sikorsky produced was the Rassky Vityas—the "Russian Knight," which became known simply as the Grand. Sikorsky's innovation was to use more than enough engines required to keep the plane aloft so that the plane would continue to fly even after one (or two) of the engines failed. More engines meant more lift, which meant larger wings, which added more weight, requiring more lift...and so on. Sikorsky's solution was a huge plane by 1913 standards: fifty-nine

The defining features of the Russian heartland—vast empty stretches and bitter cold—influenced the design of Sikorsky's planes such as the Ilya-Mourometz. These planes had enclosed cabins and long-range capability, and would stay aloft even when an engine failed.

feet (18m) long, with a wingspan of 103 feet (31.5m). The Grand made several test flights before being destroyed on the ground in a freak accident in August 1913: an engine fell off a plane passing overhead and smashed the Grand beyond repair.

Sikorsky used what he had learned to build an even larger plane: the Ilya-Mourometz (named after a mythical Russian hero), or the IM. With a wingspan of more than one hundred feet (30.5m), the IM made a historic flight in July 1914 from St. Petersburg to Kiev and back—more than eight hundred miles (1,287km) each way. The IM was initially designed for use by Russian royalty, though Czar Nicholas understood the military potential of such a machine. The IM was the first large aircraft with a fully enclosed fuselage, and the pilot's compartment was separated from a passenger cabin. With a total capacity of eighteen passengers and crew, the plane made it possible for envoys of the czar to reach far-flung areas and exert direct control over the Russian Empire.

The IMs were outfitted for comfort: they were heated, and included, incredibly, a rope-enclosed outdoor observation deck. Ten IMs were ordered, but when war broke out in August 1914, the order was increased to forty-two. The IM was the only plane of Russian origin being built in Russia, but the Dux Works bicycle factory in Moscow built many foreign planes (particularly French) under license, giving the Imperial Air Service an air force of more than 240 planes, twice the size of either France or Great Britain's, and larger even than Germany's.

The IM proved to be a remarkably sturdy plane, invulnerable to most ground fire and nearly all fighter attacks. The most obvious use for the plane was as a bomber, but very little thought had been given to the methods and tactics of strategic bombing. Although the prewar IM was outfitted with state-of-the-art instruments, the mechanisms for bomb placement and delivery were slow in coming. Another problem was maintenance: in order to be effective, the IM fleet had to carry out mission after mission from forward positions, but this was not how the plane was designed to be used. Spare parts could only be made in the Russo-Baltic plant, and the machines required trained mechanics, who were scarce.

Moreover, the Russo-Baltic plant lacked an airfield, so the planes could not be assembled there and then flown to their staging areas.

ABOVE: The Grand, the world's first four-engined airplane, made its maiden flight on May 13, 1913, piloted by its designer, Igor Sikorsky. Note the czarist emblem on the nose.

RIGHT: The immense (by 1914 standards) Ilya-Mourometz first flew a bombing mission on February 15, 1915. It could carry fifteen hundred pounds (680.3kg) of bombs and up to sixteen crew members. By war's end, a fleet of forty-two IMs flew more than four hundred missions.

They had to be crated and shipped, and then assembled in the field. This was probably the most vulnerable state the aircraft would ever be in, and several planes remained unassembled in their crates for months while new mechanics were sent to replace ones who had been killed or wounded en route. Furthermore, several planes were delayed when souvenir-hunting soldiers pocketed key parts they thought no one would miss, but without which the plane could not fly. The entire experience showed strategists on all sides that large planes were as costly and complex to maintain on the field as artillery or ground troops.

Nonetheless, the forty-two IMs that were built flew more than four hundred missions over Germany and Lithuania. During that time, only two planes were lost, an incredible record. Both the British and the French petitioned the Russians for a license to build the planes for their own bomber fleets. By then, however, Sikorsky had fled, and the Russians believed granting such a license would give the West a technological lead that would haunt them after the war. The license was never granted, and the British were unable to develop a bomber fleet before the war ended.

Chapter 7
The Vickers Vimy (U.K.)

I f the Ilya-Mourometz represented the beginning of the era of large planes, the Vickers Vimy represented its maturity. Named after a French town, the site of a Canadian victory in World War I, the Vimy was ostensibly built as a bomber capable of raiding Berlin. The Armistice cut short production, but the plane made an easy transition from wartime to peacetime use, with bomb racks and forward gunnery replaced by new fuel tanks. (Indeed, some competitors believed the transition was too easy, and accused Vickers of profiteering by using the war to develop commercial aircraft. The same charge was leveled at Sopwith, resulting in his company's eventually going under, but Vickers managed to fend off the accusations.) The Vimy had two Rolls-Royce Eagle Mark VIII engines, which produced 300 horsepower each, giving the plane great long-range capabilities and making it a contender for the Daily Mail prize offered for the first transatlantic crossing by air.

The £10,000 prize was offered in 1913 by Alfred, Lord Northcliffe, publisher of the *Daily Mail*, and was directed at sea planes, then thought to be the only planes that could possibly make it across the Atlantic. Contestants were permitted to land on the ocean, and even be hoisted onto a ship for repairs. The outbreak of war prevented anyone from pursuing the prize, and by 1919 airplane technology had accelerated to the point that a nonstop crossing could be contemplated. (In May of 1919, a group of three U.S. Navy Curtiss NC flying boats set out to cross the Atlantic. They did not compete officially for the Northcliffe Prize, and since they floated on the sea part of the way, they would not have won the contest anyway. The NC planes were, in any case, holdovers from before the war, and while the feat was hailed as heroic, the state of aviation had passed the NC planes by.)

The Vickers company shipped a disassembled Vimy to Newfoundland in thirteen large crates, along with a team of mechanics. The crates arrived on May 26, 1919, and fourteen days later the plane was ready for a test flight. Since the plane was assembled out in the

The Handley-Page V/1500 bomber, the largest deployed by the British in the First World War, was built in response to the bombing runs of the giant Gothas and the Zeppelins. Neither British nor German bombers played a decisive role in the war because they were too few in number, but strategists knew that bombers would matter in the next war.

open, in cold weather and gale-force winds, the feat was considered nothing short of miraculous, but critics of Vickers used this to buttress charges that the Vimy had been designed specifically for the Northcliffe challenge.

After two other contestants had crashed early in their attempts, the Vimy, piloted by John Alcock and Arthur Whitten Brown, took off on the morning of June 14 from an improvised airfield known as Lester's Field. After a gripping flight of sixteen and a half hours, they landed in an Irish bog, crashing the nose of the plane into the soft earth because the front landing strut had been removed to reduce weight and drag.

The success of the Vimy made it the prime candidate for conversion into a commercial air transport, particularly after its nearest competitor, the Handley Page V/1500 bomber, crashed near Cleveland, Ohio, a short time later.

The Vimy went on to complete another long-distance flight: England to Australia, a distance of more than eleven thousand miles (17,699km), in just under 136 hours in the air. The pilots, Australian brothers Keith and Ross Smith, became international celebrities, and as the 1920s began, the Vimy emboldened aircraft builders all over the world to create large planes that could transport many passengers.

LEFT: The need to assemble bombers such as the Handley-Page overseas—this one in Mitchell Field—and then ship them to the European theater made the British experts in modular construction and in transporting aircraft. BELOW: The Vimy, a modified Vickers bomber, takes off from Lesters Field in Newfoundland at the start of its historic flight.

ABOVE: The cockpit of the Vimy. Only one set of controls was handled by the pilot, while the other crew member attended to repairs and fuel matters. LEFT: The Vimy rests nose-down in an Irish bog after landing without a nose wheel, removed before the flight in an effort to reduce weight.

Chapter 8
The Ryan NYP (U.S.)

The most celebrated event in the history of flight was the product of three extraordinary aviation pioneers. One became one of the most famous people of the twentieth century: Charles Lindbergh. Another became known mainly for having given his name to the plane in which Lindbergh made his historic flight: the Ryan NYP, produced by T. Claude Ryan's fledgling aircraft manufacturing company on the fishing docks of San Diego. And the third is a man little known even to aviation enthusiasts: Charles L. Lawrence, the designer of the Whirlwind engine that powered the *Spirit of St. Louis* over the Atlantic on May 20–21, 1927.

Even though so many of the great flights of the late 1920s were possible only because of his engine, Lawrence never seemed bothered by the fact that everyone seemed to be getting rich and famous except him. He quipped, "Who ever heard of the name of Paul Revere's horse?" But when the Collier Trophy for the most outstanding contribution to aviation was awarded by the National Aeronautic Association for the banner year of 1927, it did not go to Ryan or Lindbergh or any of the other stars of that era, it was awarded to Lawrence for the development of the workhorse that made it all possible. As for Lindbergh's flight, all three visionaries had to come together if the New York–to–Paris flight was to be made.

The *Spirit of St. Louis* was born in Charles Lindbergh's mind while he was piloting mail for the Robertson brothers' private air-mail service in an old DH4, powered by the Liberty engine, about the only contribution the United States made to World War I aviation. The Liberty engines gave aircraft the range they needed to take off from England and engage the enemy over France and Germany, but they required a great deal of maintenance if they were not to fail in mid-flight.

As a long-distance air-mail carrier, Lindbergh was in a position to appreciate the importance of an aircraft's having the structural integrity necessary to carry a large quantity of fuel. It was not simply a matter of increasing power to accommodate the greater weight; the entire aircraft

The Ryan NYP, launching the illustrious careers of Charles Lindbergh and T. Claude Ryan. The absence of a forward window gave the plane a sleek, high-tech appearance, implying that navigation was accomplished by sophisticated instruments. In fact, the fuel tanks were where the pilot should have been, making a forward window unnecessary. Lindbergh used only the most primitive navigation equipment, making his flight even more remarkable.

LEFT: Ryan went on to create a series of trainer aircraft, the STs, that were the favorite trainers of WWII pilots. The ST-A shown here was among the most popular sport aircraft of the 1930s, and is considered a masterpiece of airplane design.

BELOW: the Wright-Bellanca W.B.2, the plane Lindbergh wanted to fly across the Atlantic. The plane, named *Columbia*, would prove its mettle just two weeks later by making the first nonstop flight from New York to Germany.

had to be designed for long distances. Lindbergh had probably made several flights about as long as the thirty-six hundred miles (5,792km) separating New York and Paris, and he had some definite ideas about what requirements a plane would have to meet to reliably make the flight. One such requirement was that the main fuel tank be placed in front of the cockpit so that the pilot would not be crushed by the tank in a crash.

In 1926, there was one plane that Lindbergh thought had the right design for the flight: the Wright-Bellanca W.B.2, designed by Sicilian émigré Giuseppe Bellanca, one of the greatest aircraft designers in the history of flight. Lindbergh was able to convince a group of St. Louis businessmen (who, contrary to the popular myth, knew quite a bit about aviation and were not won over simply by Lindbergh's earnestness) to finance the flight. The plan called for the purchase of the Bellanca, outfitted with Whirlwind engines. Lindbergh met with the legendary designer and the two men exchanged valuable ideas about the design requirements of the plane. But the plane fell into the hands of

ABOVE, LEFT: Outfitting the NYP with a Whirlwind engine. The Whirlwind was the engine of choice for an entire generation of aviators. In fact, the history of aviation in the late 1920s and early 1930s was the story of how other areas of aircraft technology caught up to the Whirlwind.

ABOVE, RIGHT: T. Claude Ryan was the originator of the NYP design, but he was no longer with the company when the plane was built.

financier-adventurer Charles Levine, who would sell Lindbergh the plane only if Levine could select the crew that would fly it.

In retrospect, the Wright company had all the components necessary to win the race to cross the Atlantic—the right aircraft, the right power plant, and even a visionary of Lindbergh's caliber in the person of Clarence Chamberlain, pilot and chief engineer for Wright. Most of the contestants vying for the $25,000 prize offered by Raymond Orteig, a Frenchman who had become a New York hotelier, believed the Wright-Bellanca team had the best chance, especially after disaster befell the early entrants in the race. By the spring of 1927, it was believed by those in the know that the feat would require not simply a bigger plane, but a better design. Chamberlain and Levine probably thought the prize was theirs for the taking when Lindbergh suddenly took back the $15,000 certified check he had just put on Levine's desk for the plane. What they hadn't counted on, and which (of all people) Anthony Fokker was among the first to notice, was that others were also learning from Bellanca.

ABOVE: The press, which had ridiculed Lindbergh before his flight, made him an international hero afterward. The "Lone Eagle" was tailor-made for stardom. LEFT: The throng that greeted Lindbergh as he arrived in London at the end of his historic flight was only the first of many the world over that would shower "Lucky Lindy" with accolades.

Claude Ryan had built a model, the M-2, that incorporated many features of the Wright-Bellanca W.B.2, and Lindbergh knew after just a few minutes of test-flying that a modified M-2 would do very nicely. He then worked with Ryan's chief (and only) engineer, Donald Hall, in creating the Ryan NYP ("New York–to–Paris") out of the M-2. (Ryan was not, incidentally, closely involved in this transformation. Just a month before Lindbergh's arrival, financial pressures forced Ryan to sell his share of the company to his partner B.F. Mahoney.)

Virtually every aspect of the design was examined and redesigned. Hall and Lindbergh argued over every point: whether it was wise for Lindbergh to fly solo (the Orteig prize only required that the flight be nonstop), and how he would manage taking off without forward vision, which was blocked by the large fuel tanks. A horizontal periscope was installed, but Lindbergh never used it; instead he just leaned against the side window and looked as far ahead as he could. The wingspan would have to be increased to accommodate the extra fuel, and the fuselage would have to be lengthened to accommodate the concentration of weight in the front of the plane due to the engine and the fuel. All the struts and braces of the plane were fired with aluminum or balsa wood and streamlined to reduce drag and increase control. The fuselage was welded steel, the propeller was Duralumin, a strong and light aluminum alloy, and the wheel spokes were covered with doped fabric. All the metal tubing was replaced with rubber hoses so that nothing would rattle loose from the vibrations of flight.

After an astounding two months of building, testing, and rebuilding the *Spirit of St. Louis* (as the Ryan NYP was dubbed, after its backers and Lindbergh's hometown), Lindbergh and Hall had a plane with a fuel capacity of 450 gallons (1,703L), a maximum speed of 124 miles per hour (200kph), and a range of forty-two hundred miles (6,758km) in still air. The first test of the aircraft would be getting to Roosevelt Field on Long Island, the starting point for the flight to Paris. Lindbergh flew the plane nonstop from San Diego to St. Louis in just over fourteen hours, and then to New York in seven—both incredible times.

In New York, Lindbergh waited for the weather to clear and finally received a favorable weather report while he was on his way to the theater. He got back into the car, raced to Roosevelt Field, and took off, just barely clearing the telephone wires at the end of the runway. Thirty-three and a half hours later, on Le Bourget Field, Lindbergh stepped out of his plane and into the annals of aviation history.

After Lindbergh's flight, the company (renamed the Mahoney-Ryan Aircraft Corporation) produced a successful series of planes modeled after the NYP. The company succumbed to the Depression in 1929, but Claude Ryan formed a new company, Ryan Aeronautical, and continued to produce innovative aircraft (like the STA-1, the most popular pre–World War II trainer) throughout the 1930s. For all the debt the NYP owed to the Bellanca planes, one need only look at the contestants for the Orteig prize to realize that a subtle but definite change had taken place in aeronautical design, and that the change was embodied in the Ryan NYP.

Chapter 9
The Junkers Ju-52 (Germany)

The Ju-52, brainchild of Hugo Junkers, one of the great aircraft designers of the interwar period, was an important aircraft for several reasons. It marked a high point in Junkers' career as a developer of the all-metal aircraft (in which he was the most important innovator of his day). And it served as the source for two immensely popular aircraft: the Ford Tri-Motor, or, as it was known, the "Tin Goose" (to which the Ju-52 was far superior), one of the most remarkable planes ever built, and the Fokker D-10. The Ju-52 was the airplane that allowed Germany to take the lead in civil commercial aviation in Europe. Unfortunately, and to Junkers' dismay, it also served to bolster the German military, and was, for a time, a mainstay of the reconstituted and rejuvenated Luftwaffe, a vital military arm of the Nazi war machine.

Hugo Junkers had originally been trained as a metallurgist, and he had built the J1, the first all-metal fighter aircraft, of steel and iron in 1915. It was not until 1917 that a Junkers fighter saw action: the D1, a two-seat fighter, would surely have played an important part in the war had it gone on longer. Junkers applied the most advanced principles of construction engineering to create the cantilevered wing, constructed along the same lines as the cantilevered bridge.

He was part of the German team that had developed Duralumin in 1917. Duralumin was a precursor of aluminum alloy, as strong as cold rolled steel at one-third the weight. It would certainly have been a boon to aviation, but the Germans were then committed to the zeppelin program, which used nearly all the alloy they could produce. (The formula and process for Duralumin was a closely guarded secret, and the British and Americans were unable to crack the formula even after samples had been obtained from zeppelins that had crashed in France.) In 1921, metallurgists at the Philadelphia Navy Yard developed an even better aluminum alloy. But the U.S. Navy used all the aluminum it produced to construct the frame of the ZR-1, the Shenandoah airship, instead of an airplane.

ABOVE: Hugo Junkers was the most talented German airplane designer of his generation, but his antipathy to the Nazi party and to the idea of German rearmament led to his being pushed out of his own company.

OPPOSITE: The Junkers Ju-52 was for many years the mainstay of air forces and airlines around the world. The model pictured here served in the Swiss Air Force.

Biplanes continued to overshadow monoplane designs well into the 1920s, but Junkers changed all that with little support from the German government. Throughout the 1920s, Junkers developed metal monoplane aircraft, patiently integrating ever more powerful engines into his metal aircraft, even though he was not always able to use the best grade of metal alloy available. By 1925, engines were available that made the all-metal planes as fast as comparably sized wood-and-metal planes. Still, there were several important design innovations that remained before Junkers could produce the modern airliner.

The most important of these was the placement of the wing under the fuselage. In the metal airplanes of the 1920s developed by Fokker, for example, the wing was so thick that it was necessary for the fuselage to support it with struts. This configuration was believed by Fokker's chief designer, Reinhold Platz, to be more stable—he viewed the fuselage as hanging down from the wing like a pendulum. Junkers, on the other hand, saw the entire plane as a single aerodynamic machine. His wings were strong enough to support the fuselage and he was able to create stable and controllable flight by turning up the wings and using the most advanced airfoil elements like flaps and slats. Junkers also reasoned that underwings would provide a better cushion and thus better passenger protection in the event of a crash, as well as a better opportunity to include retractable landing gear. (Junkers anticipated the possibility of the gear retracting into the wings long before it became practicable.)

The result was the Ju-52, known affectionately as Tante Ju (Aunt Ju), which served as the workhorse of Lufthansa's (the German

LEFT, TOP: The sturdy Ju-52 made very high stratospheric flight possible. Note the double propeller for greater propulsion in the thin air of the upper atmosphere. LEFT, BOTTOM: The Junkers construction technique could also be adapted to sport and racer aircraft, as in this W34, used in New Guinea before the war. OPPOSITE: With the Ju-52, airplane design and construction had clearly caught up to engine technology.

national airline) routes to Europe, Africa, and South America. The Ju-52 looked more like a modern airliner than any previous aircraft. Junkers was among the first to realize that certain aircraft configurations instill greater confidence and ease in passengers. The Ju-52 also allowed for the greatest integration of the engines into the body of the wing. (On the Fokker F-VIII, as on the Ford Tri-Motor, the side engines were connected to the bracing connecting the overwing and the landing gear.)

In fact, the only problem that resisted Junkers' engineering was the fuselage of corrugated metal, so constructed as to strengthen the body. Junkers realized that this corrugation created surface drag and diminished performance, but the planes were growing faster than engine and alloy technology could keep up. The solution to this problem was discovered by Adolph Rohrbach, a competitor of Junkers' who devised the idea of a "stressed-skin" construction in which the integrity of the frame would be borne in part by the outer skin. Rohrbach's ideas had to compete for acceptance in Europe, but found a more receptive audience in the United States when he lectured there in 1926. The later smooth-skin airliners, such as the DC-3 (built by Donald Douglas and Jack Northrop, both of whom attended Rohrbach's lectures) were based on combinations of the ideas of Junkers and Rohrback.

In the meantime, Junkers was having an influence in Germany and abroad. The Fokker all-metal airliner developed along lines remarkably similar to those appearing in the United States. Anyone who knew Anthony Fokker well would have jumped to the conclusion that it was he who had borrowed from his American competition. But this time the opposite was true: an enterprising young journalist and inventor, Bill

ABOVE: The intent of the Nazi regime to use the Ju-52 as a military plane was clear from the start. Analysts noticed, among other things, that the luggage racks were designed more for bombs than for suitcases. **LEFT:** The Ju-52 did see plenty of civilian use, of course. This diagram is of a Lufthansa Airlines Ju-52 from 1939.

The military designs on the Ju-52 were all too real, as this photo of combat Luftwaffe aircraft shows. Replaced later by the dreaded Stuka, the Ju-52 gave the Nazi air force early credibility in the eyes of many Allied analysts.

Stout, copied the Fokker designs and, through an astute publicity campaign, got a group of Detroit automobile manufacturers, led by Henry Ford, to create the Stout Metal Airplane Company. Fokker, one might say, had been out-Fokkered by the sharp young American.

Ford's initial involvement had been halfhearted; most observers believed that he was simply looking for something that would keep his ambitious son, Edsel, busy and out of his hair. But by July 1925, Ford's enthusiasm had clearly grown; he bought out the other investors and threw himself into the enterprise with gusto. After (the night after, precisely) Ford witnessed a particularly disappointing test flight of the "Air Pullman," Stout's first design, the Stout factory mysteriously and conveniently burned down.

Ford moved quickly to build a new factory and replaced Stout with a young engineer fresh out of M.I.T., James McDonnell (later to team up with Donald Douglas). McDonnell turned the Air Pullman into the 4-AT, the first Ford Tri-Motor. From 1926 to 1933, some two hundred Tri-Motors (called the Tin Goose and the Flying Washboard) were manufactured, most equipped with top-of-the-line Whirlwind or Wasp engines. Ford also built airfields and airport services for the planes. The age of commercial aviation had begun.

The competition between Ford and Fokker for dominance of the trimotor market ended in 1931, when a Fokker trimotor went down in a thunderstorm and famed football coach Knute Rockne was among the casualties. Both companies' planes were, in fact, equally safe, and both were far behind the Ju-52 technologically, but Ford was able to promote the safety of all-metal construction and boast that no Ford Tri-Motor had ever crashed due to engine failure. (This implied that the engines never failed, which was not the case. What was true was that a Ford Tri-Motor could stay aloft with only one engine working.)

Junkers was never really trusted by the German government, even during the Weimar regime, and was correctly viewed as an anti-Nazi in the 1930s, opposed to the military development of his aircraft. By 1931, Junkers was pushed aside in his own company. He died a broken man on February 3, 1935, and while Nazi propaganda claimed Junkers as their own, he would, in fact, have been horrified to have his name associated with the Stuka dive-bomber, the notorious Nazi blitzkrieg aerial weapon of World War II.

Chapter 10
The Lockheed Vega (U.S.)

ny listing of the four or five greatest aircraft of all time would certainly include the Lockheed Vega. The airplane was emblematic of the Golden Age of Flight—it was the plane of choice for the great pathfinders and the holders of the distance flight records. It represented a leap forward in aircraft design and established a number of reputations in the annals of flight. The Vega was also a testament to perseverance: the company that produced the Vega had failed twice, seen its hopes dashed by a shortsighted government, and managed to build the most advanced plane of its day without selling a single one; when the first Vega finally did roll out of the factory, it took off from Oakland, California, in a race to Hawaii—and was never seen again.

But the San Franciscans who founded Lockheed Aircraft—three brothers named Victor, Malcolm, and Allan Loughead, who in 1921 used the phonetic spelling of their Irish name as the company name—were as determined as they were talented. All three were trained as engineers and had made their mark in automobile engineering. In 1910, Allan Loughead learned to fly a Curtiss biplane, and soon the brothers were in the airplane business. Their engineering backgrounds (particularly Malcolm's) gave them an adventuresome approach to aeronautical design, and the early planes they built were valued for being the most maneuverable in the air. Victor was the author of several respected monographs on aerodynamics and remained in close contact with many of the most advanced aerodynamicists in the world throughout his life.

In 1915, the brothers built a plane in which they gave rides to visitors to the Panama-Pacific Exposition. With the $6,000 they raised, they formed Loughead Aircraft Manufacturing Company. They hired a young garage mechanic whose knack with body construction would, they felt, complement their expertise in engineering and aeronautics. His name was Jack Northrop, and he would become one of the legendary aircraft builders of the twentieth century.

The first plane the Lougheads produced was the F-1, a large seaplane that was intended for use by the U.S. Navy. The F-1 was the best seaplane available at the time, but the Navy had a strong connection to Glenn Curtiss and went with the NC planes he produced. The reason the Navy gave for turning down the Lougheads was that the technique they had devised for building the fuselage was the Lougheads' alone and could not be standardized. There was some truth to this; the process was developed largely by Allan and Northrop, and became the key to their eventual success. In 1919, Loughead used this technique to create the S-1, a single-seat biplane with tapered wings that folded so that the plane could be stored in an ordinary garage. The most remarkable part of the S-1, however, was its cigar-shaped fuselage.

Aircraft fuselage design had gone through two transitions already: from the spindly planes that were designed solely to keep the engine, wings, and pilot together, to the enclosed frame design of the World War I planes, and then again to the monocoque designs of the French in the postwar period. The Lougheads took this a step further and created the stressed-skin construction, in which the entire fuselage carried the weight as a unit.

To do this, the body of the fuselage had to be constructed out of layers of thin sheets of balsa wood that were carefully glued together and attached to a frame. (It would be some time before metal alloys were light enough to allow the fuselage to be created in a mold.) In the meantime, wood was clamped together to let the glue dry, and then the three-ply sheets were attached to the frame. It was the Lougheads' and Northrop's idea to fuse wood sheets in concrete molds and supply the pressure inside the molds with inflated balloons. Concrete molds like huge bathtubs would be lined with the sheets of wood and glued over a frame, and then a balloon would be inflated inside the mold.

The entire process took less than an hour, after which the mold would be allowed to set over twenty-four hours. Then the balloon would be deflated and the half fuselage shell would be removed. Two such shells would be connected with nails, and the basic components of an aircraft would be completed inside of three days instead of the three weeks ordinarily required.

The S-1 was quickly recognized as a great aircraft, but the end of the war had poured hundreds of virtually unused Curtiss Jenny airplanes onto the market. At a price of $30,000, Loughead was not able to sell a single plane. The company closed its doors and Malcolm returned to Detroit, where he made a fortune developing a four-wheel hydraulic brake system for automobiles. Meanwhile, Allan and Northrop (who had gone to work for Donald

One of the first Vegas to be manufactured at the Lockheed plant in Santa Barbara, California. The shock absorber system is apparent on the landing struts, but neither the NACA cowling nor the signature spatted wheel covers have become standard as yet.

Douglas) met often to kick around ideas about aircraft design and production. They knew that their manufacturing process was a real advance, confirmed when Northrop attended some of the Rohrbach lectures in 1926.

The Loughead brothers and Northrop assembled once again on the West Coast and, with additional capital from a brick manufacturer, Kenneth Jay (who insisted the company name be Lockheed), were back in the airplane business. They took the fuselage of the S-1 and added a few elements that had come their way in the intervening five years. Victor, an aerodynamicist, had kept up with developments at the wind tunnel and laboratory opened by the National Advisory Committee on Aeronautics (NACA, precursor of NASA) at Langley Field on the Virginia coast.

Some of the findings at Langley confirmed what was already known by seat-of-the-pants engineers out in the field. But one finding came as a complete surprise, and proved important in the future development of aircraft: that 30 percent of the drag experienced by an airplane was due to the exposed engine. Nearly all of this could be eliminated by placing a "cowling" (a metal cover) over the engine. Had this idea ever been entertained by any designer, it would have been dismissed for fear the cowling would interfere with the flow of air needed to cool the radial engine. But NACA showed that with just a little venting, the engine was adequately aerated and cooled.

The Lougheads took the S-1 fuselage (which could now be made of thicker plywood) and attached a NACA-cowled Wright Whirlwind engine, Malcolm's system of shock absorbers and hydraulic brakes on the landing gears, and a trim cantilevered wing that required no support struts on wires. The new plane, called the Vega, had a price tag of less than $20,000 and was state of the art the day it rolled out of the Lockheed factory on July 4, 1927.

The first Vega produced was purchased by George Hearst of the Hearst newspaper empire family. He called it the *Golden Eagle* and entered it in a race sponsored by pineapple magnate Jim Dole, who offered $35,000 to the first plane to fly nonstop from California to Hawaii. The *Golden Eagle* took off from Oakland on August 16, 1927, and was never heard from again. Several other entrants suffered the same fate, and the Dole Derby underscored the importance of planning and navigation on long-distance flights. The early Vegas were equipped with primitive navigation equipment, but in time, the explorers who favored the plane developed a full complement of devices that became standard on all the Lockheed aircraft.

The loss of the *Golden Eagle* did not adversely affect the popularity of the Vega. In fact, one explorer, the Australian Hubert Wilkins, had watched from his San Francisco hotel room as Hearst's plane took off and decided instantly that the Vega was the plane he would use to explore the Arctic. Wilkins purchased the second Vega manufactured and prepared it for a grueling flight across the Arctic Sea.

Wilkins and his pilot, Ben Eilson, took off from Point Barrow, Alaska, on April 15, 1928, and set out to cross twenty-two hundred miles (3,540km) of barren, frozen wasteland, intending to land in the

Hubert Wilkins, right, and Ben Eilson (with his foot on the landing gear) pose with the second Vega built, the plane in which the pair completed a heroic crossing of the Arctic Sea. This feat, more than any other, was responsible for the tremendous success of the Vega.

LEFT, TOP: This drawing of the cowled Vega reveals its characteristic cigar shape and spatted wheels. The standard capacity of the Vega was six passengers and a single pilot. The side-by-side copilot arrangement was not to become standard until WWII.

LEFT, BOTTOM: Wiley Post and Harold Gatty pose before the *Winnie Mae* after their grueling round-the-world flight. Post was among the few aviators who could excite the public without making his accomplishments seem like stunts.

Norwegian outpost of Spitzbergen, on the other side of the world. After some twenty hours in the air, the Vega hit a blizzard and Eilson set down on the ice. For five days the pair sat and shivered, running the plane on and off to keep the lines from freezing and to provide them with some warmth, while they lived on meager emergency provisions. Out of desperation, Wilkins got out and freed the frozen skis, and the Vega took off with only ten gallons (38L) of fuel left in the tank. Fortunately, Wilkins' navigation had been on target, and they had been forced down only five miles (8km) short of their destination. A relieved world hailed Wilkins and Eilson as heroes, and the Vega became the plane of choice for the pathfinders of the Golden Age of Flight.

By far the most famous Vega was the *Winnie Mae*, flown by Oklahoman Wiley Post. Named after the daughter of the plane's owner and Post's boss, the *Winnie Mae* was the plane in which Post and navigator Harold Gatty (also an Australian) circled the globe in June 1931. Gatty had worked closely with Gerry Vultee, the chief engineer at Lockheed (who had replaced Northrop when he left to start his own company), in creating the navigation equipment such a trip would require, including a combination ground speed and wind-drift indicator that became a standard instrument for aerial navigation.

Post and Gatty completed their round-the-world flight in just under eight days and sixteen hours, an amazing time, twelve days shorter than the *Graf Zeppelin*'s record. Two years later, however, Post (now owner of the *Winnie Mae*) completed a solo circumnavigation of the globe in twenty-one hours less, thanks to the assistance of Lawrence Sperry's autopilot (which made the trip possible, even though it failed twice in midair).

Wiley Post became world-famous, and his signature eye patch became a fashion craze of the 1930s. Post had one more celebrated flight to make. In 1934, in a pressurized suit that he helped B.F. Goodrich design for him, he took the *Winnie Mae* to fifty thousand feet (15km), establishing a new altitude record and demonstrating the feasibility of flight in the stratosphere.

The Vega was steadily improved through the 1930s, and the design was the basis for later Lockheed aircraft such as the Orion (in which Post lost his life in a 1935 crash in Alaska, which also took the life of humorist Will Rogers) and the Sirius, which became a favorite of the Lindberghs. When Jack Northrop finally produced all-metal airplanes using the techniques and data he had learned at Lockheed and Douglas, they bore a striking resemblance to the design of the Vega. Northrop was in good company, however, for the same could be said of the designs that were to emanate from Douglas, Boeing, and Focke-Wulf in the years to come.

Chapter 11
The Messerschmitt Bf 109F (Germany)

Occasionally in the history of flight (and presumably in other disciplines as well), someone comes along who takes a totally fresh look at things, refusing to be bound by older, more conventional ways of thinking. The result of this fresh approach often advances aviation science dramatically and sends it hurtling in new directions. The career of Willy Messerschmitt, builder of the most important fighter aircraft of the Luftwaffe, is a case in point.

To say Messerschmitt was precocious in the field of aeronautics would be an understatement. He founded his own aircraft company while still a teenage student in the technical high school in Frankfurt-am-Main, and built and flew a glider as his senior project. By the terms of the Treaty of Versailles, Germany was not permitted to build or experiment with powered aircraft. One way the Germans got around these restrictions was to develop engineless aircraft, or gliders. This turned out to be a boon to the German aircraft development program because gliders gave aspiring aeronautical engineers a firm grasp of the fundamentals of airfoils and aerodynamics that they would not have received working on powered machines.

Messerschmitt's small company in Bomberg was watched closely by those in Germany who hoped to rebuild an air force and re-arm Germany. Messerschmitt himself cultivated friends in the German military and took warmly to the Nazis when they came to power in 1933. He became a close personal friend of General Ernst Udet, the World War I ace who became the technical director of the Luftwaffe (though he turned on Udet when the general was made the scapegoat for the debacle of the Battle of Britain). He was equally friendly with Hermann Göring, head of the Luftwaffe, and Rudolph Hess, Hitler's deputy and himself an accomplished pilot. Messerschmitt's rise from 1926 to 1934 was no doubt engineered by Nazi sympathizers, who saw him as the likeliest developer of the fighter aircraft that the Luftwaffe could use in the coming war. By 1935, Messerschmitt had the capital to

ABOVE: Willy Messerschmitt, a man who knew how to manipulate the Nazi hierarchy in order to get his way, and who was able to get the Allies to classify him as an "unwilling participant" after the war.

OPPOSITE: The 109G-2 was one of the many variations of the basic 109 design, all of which were known simply as the Messerschmitt. Easily recognizable from the ground and in the air, the 109 was feared by Allied pilots throughout the war.

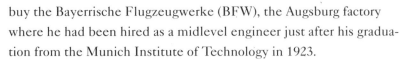

buy the Bayerrische Flugzeugwerke (BFW), the Augsburg factory where he had been hired as a midlevel engineer just after his graduation from the Munich Institute of Technology in 1923.

After his start at BFW, he soon became the chief designer and developed his earlier glider design into a sport plane, the 108 Taifun. Observers noted that the Taifun was controlled by a more powerful engine than the frame needed or could handle (at 240 horsepower, the Taifun could cruise at 165 miles per hour [265kph] and still not be at full throttle), and that the seating for four, two in the front and two in the back, was so cramped that the cockpit could easily be refitted to accommodate only two people—just the crew of a fighter aircraft. Clearly, the Taifun was a prototype for a fighter aircraft already on the drawing board.

By the mid-1930s, Germany had openly disavowed the restrictions of the Versailles Treaty, but the Nazi regime maintained a low profile in military aviation, mainly because it realized it was far behind the British, the Americans, and even the French. Göring and Messerschmitt (and the new managers at the Junkers plant, who had pushed Hugo Junkers out) embarked on a systematic campaign to rebuild the Luftwaffe and prepare it for war.

As a result, Messerschmitt enjoyed a special status in Germany. Failings that would have grounded or disqualified another manufacturer's plane were overlooked in his aircraft; his manufacturing requirements were given the highest military priority; and Messerschmitt himself was often consulted on policy questions in which aviation was relevant. It was said that Nazi involvement in the Spanish civil war was prompted mainly by the need to test Messerschmitt planes.

In 1935, the Air Ministry invited four aircraft manufacturers to compete for the contract to build the fighter that would be the foundation of the Luftwaffe fighter wing. Of the four, Messerschmitt alone was without any experience building fighters. He adapted the Taifun, putting more metal on the frame and armaments in the wing. The result was the Bf 109 (later known as the Me 109 when the name of the company was changed to MFW following Messerschmitt's purchase). From the first, the landing gear was problematic: the wheels were much too close together (which would be acceptable on a glider) for the rough terrain with which a fighter would frequently have to deal.

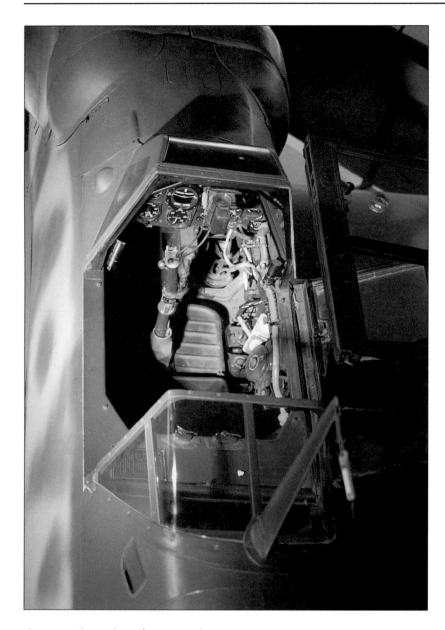

ABOVE: The cockpit of a captured Messerschmitt, illustrating the very simple controls that allowed the pilot to concentrate on flying and dogfighting. **RIGHT:** This diagram shows the Bf-109F2 flown by German ace General Adolf Galland, commander of the Luftwaffe's Squadron JG-26, as it appeared in December 1941.

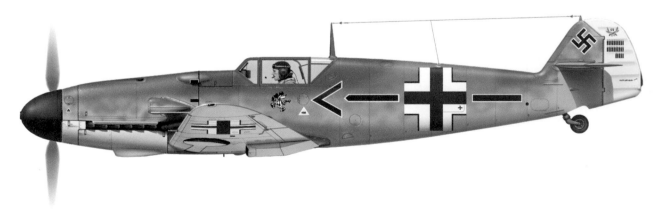

By 1944, the Bf 109F was the mainstay of the Luftwaffe. The generals realized, however, that the tradition of individualistic German aces made coordinated operations difficult, and they tried to force their pilots to stage tandem runs and overorchestrated missions. These attempts were unsuccessful, and the RAF consistently displayed a more coordinated air defense.

The engine used in the earliest Bf 109 was the Rolls-Royce Kestrel V, which was against the rules of the competition. (Not surprisingly, the judges looked the other way, though it was clear that a British engine was not going to be available for use in a German fighter that would be used in any future war against England.) At that time, however, there was simply no German engine of comparable design available.

Both Hess and Udet were nearly killed in test flights of the Bf 109, which should have put an end to Messerschmitt's career, if not his life. (In fact, German aviators would later say that for every Messerschmitt airplane design, there was a dead test pilot.) But the Bf 109 won the contest and was chosen as the plane that would become the mainstay of the Luftwaffe. Other manufacturers felt cheated, but there was little they could do about it, and they were soon given the galling assignment (or order) to build the Messerschmitt plane under license.

The first Bf 109s were flown in the Spanish civil war, where many of the plane's problems were worked out. When World War II began in 1939, the Luftwaffe had about one thousand Bf 109s. By then, the landing gear had been improved (though not to Allied levels) and a powerful German engine—the 1,175-hp Daimler-Benz DB601A—had been developed. In the early years of the war, the Bf 109 was nearly unchallenged in the sky, and the only means the British had of fighting the Messerschmitts was to devise superior strategy and tactics—at least until the Allies could put a comparable plane in the air. The same script had been played out in the First World War: the RAF had overcome the superiority of the German planes by using coordinated fighter tactics and by making certain to engage the enemy only when superior in number. As a result, the Germans had many lionized but eulogized World War I aces, and their air campaign did not alter the course or outcome of the war.

Determined not to make the same mistake again, the Germans produced the Bf 109 in huge numbers in factories all over Europe. Some thirty-five thousand planes of the 109 series were manufactured during

the war, nearly double its nearest wartime competitor, the Russian Yak-1. The version of the 109 used by the Luftwaffe in the Battle of Britain, the Me 109E (nicknamed "Emil" by the Germans), was capable of speeds of 360 mph (579kph), with a climb rate of an astounding three thousand feet (914m) per minute and a ceiling of thirty-six thousand feet (11km). These numbers were far superior to anything the Allies would put in the air until the latter stages of the war.

The Me 109E performed with lethal efficiency in the Nazi march across Europe. The German High Command was certain that the planes could establish control of the skies over England in preparation for a cross-channel invasion. (So convinced were they that they regarded the escape of a large portion of the British Expeditionary Force from Dunkirk to be of little strategic importance.) There were problems, to be sure. There was talk that the British had developed a fighter airplane based on the Schneider Cup winner, the Supermarine S6, that was a match for the Me 109E. But production of this plane had not begun until 1938, and there were still fewer than five hundred aircraft of this type in the RAF. The British fighter the 109Es would face was the Hawker Hurricane, designed by Sydney Camm. The Hurricane was a capable fighter for the mid-1930s, but no match for the 109E in head-to-head combat.

The Germans were also aware that the British had developed a system of "electronic direction-finding" (as radar was first called). They tried to learn more about it by using their commercial airliners and the *Graf Zeppelin* as spy platforms, but by the outbreak of war they were still in the dark as to how radar worked and what strategic effect it might have on the air war.

When the air campaign that became known as the Battle of Britain began in the summer of 1940, three factors combined (just barely, according to recent analysts) to ensure the German defeat. First, the British had erected an electronic wall around their southern and eastern coasts that gave them advance warning of Luftwaffe attacks. The

Germans did not believe this would be important, because they were relying not on surprise, but on the superiority of their fighters.

But the British had taken radar a step further and had constructed a command system that was connected and integrated into the radar net. The island was divided into four sectors; when an attack was detected, a coordinated force of all the fighter aircraft in the target sector responded and repelled the attackers. As a result, the superior 109Es were always fighting off larger numbers of Hurricanes. Such tac-

tics would have been foolhardy in the absence of radar and the certainty it provided that the RAF was not responding to a decoy attack and leaving large areas of the country unprotected.

The radar and communications system assembled by Sir Hugh Dowding over a ten-year period, beginning with Robert Watson-Watt's early experiments in meteorology and continuing to the establishment of a network of command posts directed from headquarters in Bentley Priory, was the real story behind the British victory. Dowding was so

LEFT: A depiction of Gunther Rall, top Luftwaffe ace, preparing for a sortie with his ground crew (schwarzmen) in the summer of 1942.

RIGHT, TOP: An enhanced version, the Me 109R, set a speed record in 1939 of 469.2 miles per hour (755 kph). RIGHT, BOTTOM: The 109 was modified and developed into many different aircraft, in some cases yielding planes that performed poorly. The 109G was adapted to desert warfare, though it never overcame the landing problems inherent in the basic 109 design.

disliked by, well, everybody, however, that most of the credit went to the fliers and to the British populace, who stoically took the pounding on the ground until the Luftwaffe was beaten back.

Second, during these engagements, the limitations of the 109 became apparent: derived from a glider design, it was hampered by its low fuel capacity and short range. The problem was not critical in the skies over Europe, but when fuel had to be expended crossing over to British skies, the low fuel load of the 109 became a serious drawback. The 109 was so limited in this respect that it could fly at full throttle for only twenty minutes before having to return to France. British pilots knew that prolonging an engagement with the 109 was as good as a hit. Flying off on an attack after a sortie run was out of the question for the 109, and it is estimated that nearly twenty percent of the 109s lost in the Battle of Britain were downed near the Channel with nearly empty fuel tanks.

The third factor that defeated the Luftwaffe in the Battle of Britain was the resolve of the British to endure the attacks until the war

was won or lost. The Nazi regime had based its strategy on its experiences in Poland and France, which was that the attacked country sued for peace (and capitulated to the Germans) the instant the strategic balance tipped in Germany's favor. Hitler was convinced that the British would cave in as soon as they lost control of the skies over England.

What would have happened if England had lost the Battle of Britain is a matter of speculation. Churchill and others insisted for many years that surrender was never an option, but theirs were not the only voices ready to be heard in England in 1940. Churchill himself realized this, and he later claimed to have had this in mind in his famous acknowledgment of the "so few" of the RAF, which makes that address all the more poignant.

As the war progressed, the 109 was developed further, reaching its peak performance parameters with the Me 109F, a plane that surpassed 400 miles per hour (644kph) with all the climb and maneuverability of the earlier models. In the long run, however, Messerschmitt's dominance turned into a liability. The 109 was laden with heavier armament, bomb loads, electronics for night flying, and even rockets. The plane went through five further major modifications, each sacrificing performance for the sake of some mission capability. Instead of developing new designs to meet these mission profiles, the Luftwaffe stayed with the 109 and hoped that the added weight would not seriously diminish performance. But these expectations were not fulfilled, and in one of the great ironies of the war, Messerschmitt's power, responsible for the building of the dreaded war machine that was the Luftwaffe, became the root cause of the defeat of the German Air Force.

Chapter 12
The Supermarine Spitfire (U.K.)

T he Spitfire was the fighter aircraft glorified by England's victory in the Battle of Britain. A close look at the critical six weeks of air engagements that formed the core of this war phase indicates that the Spitfire, while important in counteracting the most advanced German fighter, the Messerschmitt 109E, was deployed in numbers too small to be decisive. The victorious outcome was much more the product of a radar, communication, and command system decades ahead of its time.

But as the war continued, questions were raised about why the Spitfires were so late in coming. When one realizes how close England came to losing the Battle of Britain, it would seem that charges (made by, among others, Harvard senior John F. Kennedy) that England had been caught by surprise by the Nazis had some basis.

Elements connected specifically to the Spitfire, however, show that England was wary and suspicious of German intentions through the 1930s. The rise of fascism in Italy and of nazism in Germany did not go unnoticed by the British, French, and American military leaders, and all three made many quiet preparations for what they saw as a virtually unavoidable war. The political scene was certainly confusing: isolationism in the United States in the wake of the Depression, a desperate Prime Minister Chamberlain waving a sheet of paper in the hopes of sparing Britain another devastating war, and a French government riddled with corruption.

The military forces of these countries, however, were not nearly so confused or conflicted. In the United States, the scandal of congressional investigations after World War I into the mismanagement of the Liberty engine program, combined with the strong isolationism that took hold, made it appear that the United States was loath to embark on anything like a rearmament campaign. It has taken fifty years of dogged historical research for the public to learn that both England and the United States were clearly preparing for war, and that the development of advanced fighter aircraft was part of the enterprise.

The Spitfire was the most contoured, and thus the most complex, fighter aircraft built to that time. This Mk V Spitfire, armed with twenty-millimeter cannon, finally secured the skies over England, paving the way for the Allied bombing of occupied Europe.

The development of the Spitfire occurred, then, not as a happenstance, or, as has often been romantically portrayed, the product of a lone heroic designer bucking the system and the odds to produce a superior aircraft. True, the Spitfire depended on the talents and perseverance of one man, Reginald Mitchell. But military and political leaders on both sides of the Atlantic were watching Mitchell's progress and helping him every step of the way. In fact, one might say that Mitchell's inability to completely see the Spitfire through to completion, even with the resources of Vickers-Armstrong at his disposal, which necessitated his getting help from other manufacturers, accounted for some of the Spitfire's remarkable qualities. It also makes the Spitfire the first truly modern fighter aircraft from a production point of view. After the Spitfire, fewer and fewer aircraft would be produced entirely by one company; a coordinated design and manufacturing plan would involve many companies in order to produce the complex and high-performance aircraft of the postwar period.

Reginald J. Mitchell was born in 1895 and joined the Supermarine aircraft company as an engineer-designer in 1916. During the 1920s, he was chief designer of the series of planes Supermarine produced for the Schneider Cup Competition. In 1931 his S.6B retired the trophy and brought it permanently to England by winning a third consecutive victory. These races were hard-fought by the best aircraft designers and manufacturers of several nations. Many of the most intricate and subtle problems involved in high-speed monoplane design were worked out in these races. The Vickers-Armstrong company recognized the value of this experience and bought Supermarine in 1928, making sure that Mitchell came along as part of the deal.

Mitchell, a very quiet and conservative man (biographers often describe him as "tweedy"), was plagued by poor health. In 1933, he had to have most of one lung removed and he convalesced in Europe. During that summer, he met with several young German aviators who convinced him (falsely, as part of the Nazi program of intimidation

ABOVE: The forerunner of the Spitfire, the Supermarine S.6, piloted by H. Waghorn, captured the 1929 Schneider Cup. **RIGHT:** The first Spitfire squadron, No. 19, was formed in 1938. A key to Spitfire effectiveness was the fact that the plane could "scramble" at a moment's notice to meet German planes detected on radar.

through the use of disinformation) that Germany would soon have an air force of advanced fighters able to outclass anything the RAF had on the drawing boards.

Upon his return, Mitchell became a man possessed, determined to build a fighter that would give England mastery of the skies. Ignoring the doctors who kept urging him to slow down and spend the winter in warmer climes, Mitchell set about completing the fighter design he had based on his S.B, begun two

The Spitfire underwent twenty-four Mark models in the course of the war. Because every plane was built by assembling parts made by various manufacturers, planes had to be engineered carefully to fulfill performance expectations.

years earlier. The result was the F.7/30, the first plane to be called the Spitfire, but this plane was quite different from the Supermarine Schneider Cup winner. The original plane had been a seaplane (as were all the Schneider Cup entrants) that took off and landed on pontoons. To adapt the plane to land (a problem that was to confound Messerschmitt), Mitchell designed an odd gull-wing configuration that looked more like a Stuka. Mitchell was disappointed by the plane's performance—it handled well enough, but he knew better than anyone that its top speed of 238 miles per hour (383kph) was not good enough.

Mitchell went back to the drawing board and, with the desperation of a dying man, he returned to the S.6 designs and rethought every aspect of the plane, ignoring all considerations of the manufacturing capabilities of Vickers-Armstrong (or even of the entire British aircraft industry) and the availability of a sufficiently powerful engine.

The result was a compact fighter plane with sleek, sculptured lines, very small tail surfaces, and an elliptical, razor-thin wing that made it unmistakable in the sky. The power plant for the plane was an experimental Rolls-Royce engine that, as late as January 1935, had not been tested successfully. The engine's tendency to overheat was not solved until the end of the year. While Mitchell's colleague, Sydney Camm, devoted his energies to producing Hurricanes for the RAF, Mitchell designed not only the components of the plane—the most complex all-metal fighter yet produced—but also the system that would allow a large number of manufacturers to create different components for the aircraft. It was later estimated that a single Spitfire required more than 300,000 work-hours to produce, about six times the work required to produce a Hurricane.

The first test flight of the Spitfire (the RAF retained the name originally applied to the F.7/30 in spite of the fact that Mitchell detested it) took place on March 5, 1936. Vicker's chief test pilot, Matt Summers, took the plane up with Mitchell, Camm, and the Air Ministry in attendance. The instant the plane was airborne and the landing gear miraculously disappeared into the thin wings, the observers on the ground knew they were witnessing history—and quite

likely Britain's best chance at defeating the Luftwaffe. The Spitfire had a combination of speed and agility that, in the hands of a talented pilot, could outfight anything the Luftwaffe could put in the air.

Mitchell's work was far from over. Though by the end of 1936 he had had several more operations and more of his lungs and stomach removed, he worked feverishly with his assistant, Joseph Smith, to iron out all the armament problems the innovative wing design posed. Test pilots who flew the Spitfire prototypes in the winter of 1937 often reported a gray Rolls-Royce parked at the edge of the airfield—in it was Mitchell observing the test. Doctors told Mitchell he had only a few months to live, perhaps a year if he rested in a special sanitarium in Vienna. Mitchell ignored this advice until May 1937, by which time the Viennese doctors said it was too late. Mitchell died on June 11, 1937, just months before the Spitfire went into full-scale production.

The Spitfire taxed Britain's production capabilities: oddly enough, England also produced the plane considered the quickest and easiest to produce, the de Havilland Mosquito. That more than twenty thousand Spitfires were produced during World War II, even during periods of German bombardment, was one of the truly amazing feats of the war. By the time the Battle of Britain was in full swing, fewer than a quarter of the squadrons needed to counter the Bf 109s were deployed: the slack would be picked up by the heroic pilots of the Hurricanes.

The question has often been raised: which was superior, the 109 or the Spitfire? At the start of the war, the 109 was faster, particularly at higher altitudes, and could both dive and climb faster; the Spitfires turned and maneuvered better, were more durable and better armed, had longer flight times, and were easier (only slightly) to master. Most early head-to-head confrontations ended in a draw.

The development of the Merlin engine and later the Griffon engine, however, led to improved versions of the Spitfire, while efforts to improve or widen the mission profiles of the 109 sacrificed too much of that plane's performance. By war's end, the Spitfires were clearly dominant in the sky, though not without significant challenge from another Luftwaffe plane, the upstart Focke-Wulf FW 190.

ABOVE: The Spitfire was able to carry bombs and rockets, in addition to machine guns and cannon, without sacrificing much of its flight characteristics. LEFT: In 1944, the Mk XII model Spitfire appeared. It had clipped wings to increase its maneuverability to the level of the Me 109.

Chapter 13
The Douglas DC-3 (U.S.)

t's hard to imagine a list of great airplanes short enough to omit the DC-3. The impact of the DC-3 on aviation history is difficult to gauge; in one bold stroke it made air travel an option that ordinary people (with ordinary stomachs for the trauma of flying) could consider. By the early 1930s, the rail and highway system crisscrossing the United States was quite well developed, and people could travel in safety and comfort without subjecting themselves to the risk, discomfort, and expense of air travel.

To be sure, some progress had been made in air transports. By 1930, the design innovations of Hugo Junkers and Adolf Rohrbach had been applied to create an impressive array of planes. Junkers pioneered the use of the cantilevered wing and all-metal Duralumin construction; the result was the Junkers Ju-52, the 1932 culmination of a design chain begun in 1919 with the Junkers F-13; it was a sleek trimotor with a corrugated metal body that rested atop the wide, swept-back wings. The Ju-52 was the cornerstone of Lufthansa, and was used extensively throughout World War II. Rohrbach eventually developed a technique for "stretching" the aluminum over a framework, which eliminated the need for drag-producing corrugation.

Two manufacturers who adopted the ideas of Junkers and Rohrbach, albeit imperfectly and inconsistently, were Anthony Fokker, who built the single-engine Fokker F-VII in 1924 and later the trimotor F-10, and William Stout, who built the Ford Tri-Motor, or Tin Goose. These planes carried twelve passengers in elegantly appointed cabins, but there was no getting around the noise (passengers had to shout to be heard), the vibration, and the slow speed (about 105 miles per hour [169kph]). The fact that these planes were not pressurized forced them to fly low and made them subject to weather conditions, which meant a bumpy ride even in good weather; if they flew high to cross mountains, the temperature and oxygen level in the cabins dropped uncomfortably low. In spite of the strides made, only the hardiest (and most impatient) of travelers opted for air transportation.

The DC-3 was the crowning achievement of the first third of the century of aviation. It became symbolic of America's ascendancy as a superpower and as a technology leader. This DC-3 was the plane used by the president of the United States as Air Force One.

The course of commercial aviation came to a crossroads on the morning of March 31, 1931. Over a Kansas farm a Fokker F-10A Tri-Motor operated by TWA (which then stood for Transcontinental and Western Airlines) encountered turbulence from a storm that had just passed through. The pilot was on the radio to Wichita requesting weather information and was considering climbing. A farmer below watched the plane pass overhead—flying at six hundred feet (183m) it would have been quite loud—and then returned to his chores. He suddenly heard the motor sputter and he looked up. He saw the F-10A fall to the ground like a stone, with a wing missing. The plane hit the ground with a thud, and the missing wing could be seen drifting to earth a quarter mile (402m) away. In other trimotor crashes, the fuel tank would rupture and there would be a great explosion and fire that would reduce the wreckage to ashes. But this time the combination of the pilot's quick thinking, shutting down the engines before impact, and the soft, muddy earth of the cornfield prevented the explosion. For the first time, Department of Air Commerce (DOAC) investigators could examine the wreckage carefully and determine what had happened.

Ordinarily, the crash would have made the front pages for a few days and then would have passed out of the public eye. It would not do the image of air transportation any good, but the airlines were already adept at managing the damage of such a story. The public perception of air travel would not have suffered much. But this crash was different for two reasons: first, one of the eight people killed in the crash was famed Notre Dame football coach Knute Rockne, and second, the reason for the crash was easy to determine. It had not been ice on the wings or a bomb planted by disgruntled gamblers, as had been rumored. The DOAC determined that the wing-root, the connection between the wing and the fuselage, made of a combination of wood and metal, had broken off because the wood had rotted away, due, presumably, to constant exposure to weather.

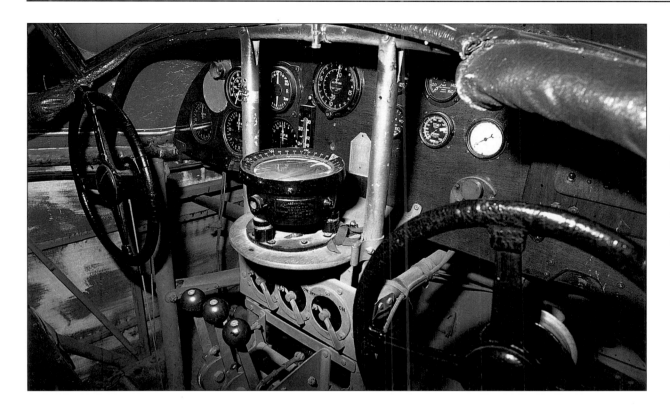

Fokker moved quickly to contain the damage, and offered to have all F-10s dismantled to check for rotted wood or anything else that might be wrong. (The fact that nothing short of dismantling the entire plane would have revealed the rotted wood in the wing certainly had a disquieting effect.) The Fokker planes had, after all, an excellent reputation for safety and performance. But the story was too big, as was the grief and outcry over the death of Rockne, and Fokker never recovered in the United States. Many airline executives realized that a much improved plane was needed if the average citizen was ever going to consider air travel.

Such a plane, as it happened, was already in the works. Several designers—most notably Jack Northrop at Lockheed and Claire Egtvedt at Boeing—had studied Junkers and Rohrbach a bit more carefully and had created several highly praised and financially successful all-metal aircraft. Northrop became a virtual celebrity for having designed the Lockheed Vega, and Boeing had established itself as the most technologically advanced aircraft manufacturer with the Monomail, a single-engine, stressed-metal-skin mail carrier with an engine cowl (collar) and retractable landing gear to reduce drag. Now Boeing was developing a state-of-the-art air transport that would give it a forward position in the market.

With the grounding of the F-10s following the Rockne crash, TWA's twenty-nine-year-old vice president Jack Frye joined the scramble to find a replacement aircraft. He approached Boeing and offered to order its new plane, the 247, even though it had not yet been completely designed, let alone flight-tested. Boeing, however, was at that time part of a larger corporate entity that included United Airlines. Though they would never admit to any collusion, the Boeing execu-

tives told Frye they would be glad to fill TWA's order after they had filled United's order for sixty airplanes, which would mean two years after the 247 had joined United's fleet. TWA did not have two years: it was barely keeping afloat in 1932, and by 1934 would probably no longer need planes of any kind.

There were also some things about the way the 247 was developing that bothered Frye. Boeing confidently kept the media aware of its progress in developing the 247. The entire aviation community was aware that the weight of the plane had been reduced from sixteen thousand to twelve thousand pounds (7,264 to 5,448kg), that the 600-hp Hornet engines had been replaced by less powerful Pratt & Whitney Wasp engines, and that the plane's cruising and landing speeds (155 and 60 miles per hour [249 and 96kph], respectively) were 10 percent lower than originally designed. Most significantly, however, the passenger load of the 247 turned out to be ten, which was even less than the F-10. It seemed to Frye that Boeing was headed in the wrong direction.

Also, Egtvedt made a design decision on the 247 that was to haunt him for many years. In order to emphasize the integrity of the wing and contrast the 247 with the F-10, he placed a wing spar through the lower half of the fuselage. Passengers walking down the center aisle of the plane had to step over a two-foot (61cm) hump in the middle of the plane. Whether this spar (and its placement) was necessary, as Boeing claimed, was hotly debated in aeronautic circles, but its effect was to make the 247 seem less spacious and less comfortable than even the Tin Goose.

In August 1932, Frye sent letters to several aircraft manufacturers expressing TWA's desire to purchase ten or more transport aircraft with the following specifications: they had to be all metal, except for those elements and appointments where metal was less preferable; weigh about fourteen thousand pounds (6,356kg); and have a cruising speed of more than 150 miles per hour (241kph), a top speed of 185 mph (298kph), but a landing speed of no more than 65 miles per hour (104kph). They had to carry at least twelve passengers and a crew of two and have a range of at least 1,080 miles (1,737km). Frye preferred a trimotor design because it seemed to lessen the chance of a crash due to engine failure. Aware that Boeing had opted for a twin-engine design, however, he allowed for that option, but stipulated that each plane's performance had to be unaffected when one engine was shut down, including taking off and landing at airports several thousand feet above sea level (where the rarefied air provided less lift).

At the last moment, TWA's technical consultant Charles Lindbergh added an additional requirement, one that the 247 would probably not have been able to fulfill: the plane had to be able to climb with one engine cut and maintain a level flight higher than the highest mountain on TWA's routes. There was no mention in Frye's letter of what TWA was willing to pay for such a plane.

One of Frye's letters was sent to Donald Douglas, then forty years old and a highly respected designer and builder, mainly of military aircraft. Much has been written about why Douglas took up Frye's challenge. It was clearly not because his company needed the business: as wildly successful as Douglas was in commercial aviation, it would be more than twenty years before that area accounted for half the business Douglas was doing with the military. Besides, the country was in the midst of the Depression and it was difficult to see a need for a plane that would make flying acceptable to ordinary people—most of whom could not afford it.

The letter had been sent to other companies that had a bigger stake in commercial aviation. Besides, why take on Boeing when it had a guaranteed success in the 247 because of its connection with United? Then again, Boeing's crowing about the 247, and the backroom whisperings about Boeing's shabby treatment of Frye, may have been just the kind of things to rouse Douglas' competitive juices.

The Boeing 247 in 1933. The company had every right to believe its aircraft was state-of-the-art, but that clearly would not have been enough to change public attitudes about air travel.

He may also have seen this as a way of utilizing two powerful resources he had recently acquired: the talents of Jack Northrop, now at his disposal by virtue of Douglas' having bought 51 percent of the stock in Northrop's company, and the technical expertise and laboratory facilities of scientists at Cal-Tech like Clark Milikan and Arthur Klein, with whom he had developed a special rapport. Aware of how important the training he and his chief aeronautical engineer, Arthur Raymond, had received at M.I.T. was, Douglas may have hoped he could gain a competitive edge by establishing a research program more advanced than NACA, the research of which was, after all, government funded and thus public.

Douglas conferred with Raymond and two of his other stalwarts, James H. "Dutch" Kindleberger, his chief industrial engineer, and Harry Wetzel, his general manager. All three told Douglas they doubted if such a plane could be built; all three wondered why Douglas was interested in trying to build one. A few days later, Douglas informed the group that he had made an appointment with Frye and the executives at TWA in New York to present the proposal for a plane that would meet or exceed Frye's requirements—a proposal they did not as yet have. Not wishing to let on that the team, particularly Raymond, needed more time, he told Frye that the group was coming to New York by train because some of the members of his team were still fearful of flying after the Rockne crash—a story Frye almost certainly did not believe.

On the train, Raymond worked round the clock as the entire team feverishly prepared the details of the proposal. They finished almost as the train was pulling into Penn Station. The group proceeded directly to TWA's offices and presented the proposal to Frye, his executives, and Lindbergh. To some who attended the meeting, it seemed that Lindbergh was skeptical, perhaps even a bit hostile. New requirements were set forth, this time having to do with maintenance: it had to be possible for a single mechanic to remove and replace the entire landing gear in an hour, or a fuel tank in thirty minutes, and so on. Each requirement in and of itself made perfect sense; taken together, they represented a new level of planning and engineering in aviation.

On September 30, 1922, TWA signed an agreement to buy a test model of the plane—now called the DC-1, for "Douglas Commercial"—and vaguely promised to buy as many as sixty more. There was still no mention of price. Douglas may have believed he was in a competitive situation, unaware that none of the companies to whom Frye had sent his letter showed any inclination to meet his challenge, for all of the above stated reasons, and one other reason: they knew TWA could not afford such a plane. Douglas was also aware of this, but he had long come to recognize that, if there is one thing for which airline executives had consistently shown an uncanny talent, it was for raising quick cash.

When the team returned to Santa Monica (they had no trouble flying back on a Fokker F-10), they set about designing, testing, and perfecting every aspect of the plane. It was largely Raymond's idea to

The success of the DC-3 can be measured by the fact that by 1938 the plane carried 95 percent of U.S. air traffic. Civil and military air operations around the world, such as the Royal Australian Air Force, clamored for the DC-3.

The effect of the DC-3 was felt throughout the aviation industry, insofar as it raised the professionalism expected of pilots, ground crews, and airport facilities.

design the plane from the potential passenger outward, instead of fitting the passenger in the available space after the plane was finished. Mock cabins were built, and chair designs tested. An upholstered chair with an adjustable back- and footrest was chosen. Care was given to the heating, venting, and soundproofing, and to the lavatories and galley. The same approach was taken with the cockpit and with all the equipment. Tests of the control panel configuration led to an ergonomic design, and everything from the seat belt buckle to the coffeemaker was redesigned. The result was a cabin that was spacious and comfortable, yet economical and modern.

Once the people—passengers and crew—were taken care of, the designers turned to the wings, the power plant, and the rest of the plane. Here, Northrop was the key designer—his importance was indicated by the fact that he was the only member of the DC-1 team mentioned by name in the TWA contract, and whose involvement in the contract was a condition of the deal. Northrop had taken the monocoque design to its ultimate conclusion, creating a wing and fuselage that were virtually indestructible. The surfaces were tested with weights, pulleys, and even steamrollers without showing any signs of buckling. During one test flight, the pilot forgot to lower the landing gear, and the plane flopped on its underside and skidded down the runway, coming to a halt amid a shower of sparks. The landing would have demolished any other aircraft, but on the DC-1 there was hardly a scratch on either the fuselage or the wings. The wings were flexible, a fact that alarmed passengers when they saw them flapping in flight. But this flexibility actually increased the wing strength. (Ever conscious of the importance of public perception, the team discussed whether to do away with this flexibility. In the end, the added strength

and the safety it provided would, it was believed, override the unnerving effect of the flapping wings.)

Very sophisticated wind tunnel tests were conducted at Cal-Tech to determine the best wing configuration. The larger size of the plane made it difficult to design a wing that would lower the landing speed to the required 65 miles per hour (104kph). The solution was to introduce the most advanced combination of flaps and slats on the front and rear edges of the wing to slow the plane down. Raymond believed that the additional weight of the highly developed landing gear would make it possible for the plane to land safely at higher speeds, but Douglas insisted that the condition be met, and it was.

The added weight caused by the generous passenger appointments required a larger wing and more powerful engines. The engines selected were a pair of 710-hp Wright Cyclones. (Like Boeing, Douglas favored a twin-engine to a trimotor configuration.) The wings were so large that stability problems were encountered until the wing was swept back and the nacelles carrying the engine were fared into the wing seven feet (2m) forward of the wing's leading edge. The effect was dramatic, and the stability was so unexpectedly high that the plane virtually flew itself once aloft. The upward tilt of the DC-1 was a happy accident that was unnecessary but which gave the plane an ultramodern look. It was retained in later DC models.

A number of important innovations, which became standard in subsequent air transports, were incorporated into the DC-1: flaps on the forward and rear edge of the wings that cut down landing speeds; an advanced landing system operated by hydraulics; variable-pitch propellers that adjusted automatically to wind speed; and a totally pressurized, soundproofed, and climate-controlled cabin and cockpit.

On July 1, 1933, the DC-1 was unveiled on a pier in Santa Monica. It was larger than the 247 and seemed almost mythical, glistening in the California sun. A British reporter covering the event thought the plane was a prop for a futuristic science fiction movie. The plane was eighty-five feet (26m) from wing tip to wing tip, eleven feet (3.5m) wider than the 247, and sixty feet (18m) long—nine feet (3m) longer than the 247. It weighed 17,500 pounds (7,945kg), nearly five thousand pounds (2,270kg) more than the 247. Thanks to its systematic cabin design, the DC-1 could accommodate fourteen passengers, two more than Frye had specified. The rigorous testing that followed showed that the DC-1 could not only perform magnificently, it could do so even with a single engine (pleasing even Lindbergh), and could be fully maintained (practically disassembled and then reassembled) by one or two maintenance people at low cost.

Only one DC-1 was produced; the model ordered by TWA for commercial use was its successor, the DC-2. The surest sign that the DC-2 was the passenger aircraft of the future was the fact that Fokker paid Douglas handsomely for the European rights to the plane.

Douglas was filling orders as fast as his factory could turn out the planes, when, in 1934, C.R. Smith, president of American Airlines, which had a large number of DC-2s, approached him and convinced him (pestered him, really) to enlarge the DC-2 so that it could be used as a transcontinental sleeper carrier. Douglas reluctantly turned the matter over to his

Though it was thought at first that the DC-3 would eliminate small airlines (since only large companies could afford the plane), the exact opposit occurred, because now a larger portion of an airline's operating budget was in the air

engineers, and the result was a larger version of the DC-2, the DST or "Douglas Sleeper Transport," a plane with sleeping berths for fourteen passengers.

Refitted as a day flier, the DST became a twenty-one-passenger plane, the DC-3. The DC-3 became the first transport that was profitable without a government mail subsidy. By 1939, a full 75 percent of the entire U.S. commercial air traffic was carried on DC-3s; airports across the country seemed to service virtually nothing else.

The DC-3 became a plane about which legends were bound to arise. In many cases, the tall tales did not adequately describe its capabilities and durability. Many cases are on record of crash landings, crashes into mountainsides, midair collisions, even bombs going off in the luggage compartment, and the plane not only discharging its passengers safely, but also returning to service soon after minor repairs. Of the eleven thousand DC-3s manufactured from 1939 to 1949, three-fourths were used for military transport: the U.S. Army's C-47, the Navy's R4D, and England's Dakota. The low transport fatality rate during World War II was certainly due to the excellence of the DC-3.

Douglas was awarded the Collier Trophy in 1935 for his contribution to aviation by developing the DC-2. Unlike other Collier award ceremonies, this one was conducted by President Franklin D. Roosevelt in the White House. It was clear to many people as early as 1935 that Donald Douglas had changed the course of aviation history.

Chapter 14
The Mitsubishi A6M-3 Reisen—the Zero (Japan)

The name Jiro Horikoshi is not widely known, even among aviation enthusiasts; his is certainly not a name one would place among the likes of Douglas, Hawker, Mitchell, and Messerschmitt when listing great designers of military aircraft. Yet Horikoshi certainly deserves that honor, since it was he who designed the most important fighter aircraft of the Japanese Air Force of World War II: the Mitsubishi A6M-3 Reisen, given the military designation ZEKE and known as the Zero (after the Japanese designation of the aircraft as "Type 00").

One possible reason more is not said or written about Horikoshi (besides the fact that little documentary material has so far come to light) is that his story is something of an embarrassment to the United States, a reminder of a monumental miscalculation.

In 1930, the United States was grappling with an economic depression that gripped the entire world. Looking at the world situation from a long-range point of view, it seemed to most military planners that the country was on a collision course with the Soviet Union. The United States looked for possible allies in what was considered an inevitable confrontation, perhaps even a war, between the forces of capitalism and the forces of communism. The situation was further confused by the presence of other forms of government that would play a role in the conflict: monarchy in Japan and fascism on the rise in Italy and Germany. In the minds of the analysts, and even many American and British leaders, an alliance with the two outer neighbors of the Soviet Union, namely Germany and Japan, could prove useful in any future confrontation. That World War II saw the United States and Britain allied with the U.S.S.R. and at war with both Germany and Japan is one of those ironic turns of which history is so fond.

Believing that it was in its own interests to bolster Japan's military capabilities, particularly in aviation, the United States arranged for a Japanese "inspector" to have free access to several aircraft manufacturing plants in the United States. Jiro Horikoshi was assigned to the

The appearance of the Zero came as a rude surprise to American military analysts who for years had dismissed capabilities in aviation technology. The Zero was so light and nimble that it could carry a bomb load and disposable fuel tanks while still being able to engage Allied fighters.

Curtiss-Wright plant on Long Island, where he carefully observed and absorbed the methods of American aviation technology. (It has been speculated that other such inspectors were placed elsewhere, sometimes without the knowledge of the manufacturer.) Horikoshi toured other plants in the 1930s; he was probably the most knowledgeable non-American individual on American military aviation. He was, by all accounts, an affable young man, and he claimed, right to his death in 1982 at the age of seventy-eight, that he was a great admirer of the United States and was troubled throughout the war about his role in arming Japan.

When Horikoshi returned to Japan, he became chief engineer of Mitsubishi. The company's aviation division was the most advanced in Japan, but was still considered twenty years behind the West. That would put its aircraft in the pre–World War I category, which is an accurate description of Japanese aviation prior to Horikoshi's return. The governments of the United States, England, and Germany, along with investors from all three countries, backed Mitsubishi's efforts to upgrade its manufacturing capabilities. The result was Horikoshi's A5M, unveiled in 1935 (in a ceremony that included dignitaries from the three countries that had made it possible), the world's first carrier-based, all-metal monoplane fighter.

The A5M catapulted Japan into the first rank of military air powers. The plane was amazingly agile; most Western pilots were unable to master the maneuvers that were required of all Japanese pilots. The A5M was used by the Japanese in China in 1937, by which time American support of Japan had changed to apprehension about Japanese intentions in the Pacific.

The specifications for the next-generation Japanese fighter were submitted by the Japanese Navy to Mitsubishi and its chief rival, Nakajima, in 1937. It was clear that only Mitsubishi had the capability to create what would be, if built to these specifications, the best-performing fighter in the world. The Japanese military hoped the chal-

lenge would raise Nakajima to the level of Mitsubishi, so that Japan would then have two sources of high-performance military aircraft. Though the exercise did turn Nakajima into a producer of quality military aircraft, this fighter was beyond its capabilities, and the field was soon left to Mitsubishi.

The fighter the navy wanted was to have a top speed of 310 miles per hour (499kph) at thirteen thousand feet (4km); a climbing rate of one thousand feet (305m) per minute; and a flying range of eight hours, with two hours of combat capability and room for auxiliary fuel. This last requirement was known to the West, and was a certain tip-off that the Japanese intended to use the plane far from its islands; not a few worried eyebrows in Western capitals were raised. The A6M was unveiled in 1939.

Horikoshi's design philosophy represented a blend of the American and the Japanese. All the Mitsubishi planes were regarded by their Japanese pilots as extensions of the weapons of the samurai. This meant that airplane designs emphasized agility and accuracy, setting aside questions of protection and durability. Warriors were, after all, supposed to fend for themselves or learn to absorb blows and continue

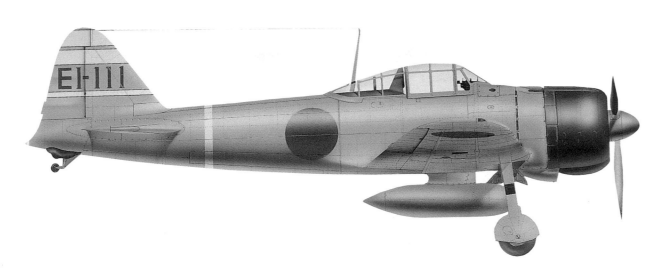

ABOVE: A special Allied unit based in Brisbane, Australia, assembled a complete Zero from the remnants of downed planes. The Zero was so simple a machine that, for some time, analysts working with the unit could not believe that a complete plane had been assembled. LEFT: An illustration of the Zero flown by celebrated Japanese ace Hideki Shingo.

on. While the British were installing bulletproof glass in their fighters and the Americans were plating their planes in steel, the Japanese were producing a light plane—rarely more than six thousand pounds (2,724kg)—that depended on its agility to evade ground and air fire.

This approach accounted for the great success of the Japanese in the first two years of the war as they expanded across the South Pacific and attacked Pearl Harbor. But it was also the source of the plane's weakness. Adversaries knew about the Zero's poor protection and tried to outlast it in the air. Inferior Curtiss P-40 Hawks, which stood no chance in one-on-one combat with Zeros, swarmed and traded hits, and often fought the Japanese to a draw.

Horikoshi responded by modifying the A6M, upgrading its armament, armor, and power plant. By

The Zero spurred an American development program to create more agile aircraft. The P-38 Lightning, seen here giving chase to a Zero, was a prime example of a nimble plane with ample protection and firepower.

contrast, the Allied response to a need for improved fighter performance was to build a new fighter. But the Allies had many manufacturers capable of advanced fighter design; Japan had only Mitsubishi. As a result, faster and heavier models of the A6M rolled off the assembly lines. In all, nearly twelve thousand A6Ms were produced during the war, more than any other Japanese aircraft—even when it was clear the plane was outclassed by American planes like the P-38 Lightning and the P-51 Mustang, arguably the best fighter of the Pacific war.

The standard, however, had been set by the Zero. The agility of the Zero forced the Allies to devise aerial tactics that would not be fully appreciated and used until jet fighters came into use after the war.

Chapter 15
The Yak-3
(U.S.S.R.)

An unfortunate by-product of the Cold War has been the utter confusion among aviation historians—and spreading from there to the general public—about the role of air power in Soviet skies during World War II. Pronouncements by the Soviet propaganda machine about their achievements in aviation were so transparently chauvinistic that it was difficult to distinguish between reasonable and legitimate claims on the one hand and absurd and false claims on the other. The politicization of fact, coupled with the Soviet penchant for secrecy, has obscured both the achievements and failures of the Red Air Force in World War II.

One of the facts that has been lost is that the eventual success of the Red Army in preventing the Nazi conquest of Russia owed much to the development and deployment of a single fighter aircraft, the Yak-3, at a crucial and pivotal moment in the war. An inescapable fact is that in 1943, during the complex series of engagements and maneuvers known collectively as the Battle of Kursk, had the balance of power on the battlefield not been tipped in favor of the Russians by the appearance of the Yak-3 in the skies, the Nazi attempt to shore up its defenses in the Caucasus (in what the Nazis called Operation Citadel) would have succeeded, giving Germany a defensible position in Eastern Europe. This would have allowed the Wehrmacht access to the oil fields of Russia and let Germany mount a much more vigorous defense against the Allied invasion of Sicily. Some historians point to the repulsion of the Nazis on the outskirts of Moscow as a key turning point in the war, while others point to the failure of the Nazis to break the siege of Stalingrad. In both operations, air power played crucial roles, but not because the Red Air Force mounted a credible challenge to the Luftwaffe; instead, as was the case during the first two years of war between Germany and the Soviet Union, the resistance encountered by the Wehrmacht amounted to the kind of strategy a boxer being pummeled uses against an opponent beating him senseless: he hopes to wear his adversary out before he is beaten to death.

The Yak-3 was as great an achievement in industrial engineering as it was in aeronautical engineering, because it had to be produced under incredibly adverse conditions. So good a plane was the Yak-3, in fact, that it was used against U.S. jet aircraft in the Korean War, though without great success.

LEFT: Göring's Luftwaffe found the Stuka so useful and dependable that research into more advanced aircraft was neglected during much of World War II. BELOW: S.V. Ilyushin was one of several young Soviet aircraft designers who were forced by circumstances to try out new designs aggressively in an effort to catch up with Germany's air capabilities.

The military engagements between Germany and the Soviet Union during this period often amounted to the Germans advancing and achieving nearly any military objective they set for themselves, being slowed only by the retarding forces of nature—weather, terrain, and fire—and the tenacious resistance of the poorly equipped Red Army. In his reports back to Berlin, Luftwaffe Field Marshal Kesselring often described operations against the Russians as "infanticide." Realizing the war with fascism was a matter of life and death for his country and for communism, Stalin rejected any possibility of surrendering to Hitler. This was in marked contrast to the rest of Europe, where all the countries capitulated once the military confrontation was decided on the battlefield.

The same was true of the war in the air. The planes used by the Red Air Force were years behind the Luftwaffe's; the front line included a biplane, the Polikarpov I-153, that would have been an excellent fighter—in the previous war. The Soviet bureaucracy gave Nikolai Polikarpov such power, however, that the I-153 kept being produced into the 1940s. An outcry from younger designers only resulted in Polikarpov consenting to produce a monoplane, the I-16, whose primary use was ramming enemy aircraft and causing both planes to go down in flames.

The Red Air Force also labored under several handicaps that made it impossible for it to mount a serious challenge to the Luftwaffe. Stalin believed the only role the air force would play was as support for ground troops. As a result, planes were thought of as flying tanks, and most were overarmored and underpowered. Another result was that Russian airfields and aircraft factories were placed in forward military positions so that the planes would be near the front lines. This was tactically foolish, as it made the entire air force vulnerable to quick attack. Stalin pointed to Hitler's blitzkrieg tactics for support for this policy, but there were, in fact, nearly no similarities between the Luftwaffe and the Red Air Force, a fact stated clearly by none other than Charles Lindbergh, who toured and reviewed both extensively.

To make matters worse, the Red Air Force was undergoing a complete restructuring when Germany invaded on June 22, 1941, and was in a near-total state of confusion for many months afterward. Following a series of purges of the Red Air Force High Command, Alexander Novikov, a young infantry officer with little aviation experience, was made commander of the air force. Novikov had an uncanny ability to manipulate the Politburo and Stalin; luckily, he also had a clear idea of how best to use his resources—limited in technical capability, but numerically superior.

Novikov had two main aircraft with which to work: the Ilyushin IL-2 Shturmovik, and the Mikoyan-Gurevich MiG-3. Both planes were deeply flawed and could not measure up to their counterparts in the Luftwaffe, the Stuka and the Bf 109, respectively. Novikov accepted this and devised strategies that would give his forces some measure of effectiveness, even against better aircraft. Planes were used only as support for ground troops and with heavy ground support from anti-aircraft fire. The Soviet planes flew only in large groups (sometimes too large, making it easy for German fighter pilots to hit them), and only with weather and terrain on their side. For example, Russian aircraft were built to land on rough dirt airfields that chewed up the landing gear of German planes. The Shturmoviks were given additional armor that virtually made them into flying tanks, with a durability estimated at one hundred times that of a Stuka.

In order for these strategies to work, Novikov had to keep plane production high (to replace the many shot down), and had to hope the front would remain a long one, making it impossible for the Germans to concentrate their formidable air power. He knew that sooner or later, however, there would come a day of reckoning when all these measures would not suffice and Russia would prevail only if it could achieve at least some parity in the air.

Solving the first problem, producing enough aircraft, was not going to be easy. To bolster the economics of Eastern European satellite states, Stalin had placed many of the manufacturing plants in the west, which made them vulnerable. Hitler, in fact, believed the war with Russia was over as soon as he learned the factories had been successfully bombed. What he did not count on was the Russians staging a massive relocation effort, dismantling and moving thousands of factories, tens of thousands of tons of raw material, and millions of workers, all transported east of the Urals—in many instances fleeing just hours before German bombs leveled the empty shells of the factories. Trainloads of freezing workers and their families arrived in the middle of winter to find local peasants still building their dormitories. It was an incredible and desperate effort which the Germans did not believe

could be pulled off. At first, it seemed even to the Russians that it could not be done, but a remarkable young aircraft designer stepped forward and organized the new factories, leading them to greater production levels—and creating better quality planes—than they achieved when back in the west. His name was Alexander Sergeivitch Yakovlev. He was born in Moscow on March 19, 1906, to an aristocratic family and received the excellent education typical of the privileged classes even after the revolution. While studying aeronautical engineering at the Soviet Air Force Academy, he became friends with Sergei Ilyushin; the two men, sometimes working together, sometimes independently, would develop many of Russia's most important military aircraft for the next several decades.

Yakovlev was, by all accounts, a bon vivant who liked wild parties, fast cars, and beautiful women. He was also a charming individual who knew how to ingratiate himself with Communist Party leaders. (He became a friend of a minor party official whom he believed would one day rise to the top of the Politburo: Nikita Khrushchev.) Yakovlev so impressed Stalin at an air show in 1935 that he was afforded the unheard-of honor of being sent to inspect aircraft industries all over Europe. He took special note of the work being done at the Hawker-Armstrong plant where the Hurricane and Spitfire were being developed, but was singularly unimpressed by the BFW plant, which had just been taken over by Messerschmitt.

In 1938, Yakovlev was invited to enter a competition for a new Soviet fighter. He won the contest, the Order of Lenin, 100,000 rubles, and a new car. His plane, the I-26, was a light, armed version of a series of sport planes he had been designing for more than a decade. In production, the plane was designated the Yak-1.

The German invasion took place just as the Yak-1 was going into production. Yakovlev personally supervised the dismantling of his factories and the relocation of his workers, all the while refining the design. He realized that the planes he would be producing east of the Urals had to be different from the ones he had begun to build in the west. They had to be simpler (spare parts were simply not going to be available), easier to fly (well-trained pilots, too, would be scarce), and able to accept a variety of armament, since there was no way of knowing what would be produced in the new factories.

The result was the Yak-9, a light and simple fighter that was agile, relatively fast, and able to fend off German fighter attacks, especially if given any numerical or tactical superiority. The Yak-9 was also a very versatile and rugged plane that gave the Red Air Force the first hint that it might be able to contend with the Luftwaffe for control of the Russian skies.

The moment of truth Novikov had both feared and hoped for came in early July 1943. After two frustrating years fighting the Russian winter and Russian resolve, Hitler decided to forego the bold stroke and listen to his generals. For the first time in the war, the front lines showed a salient in the Kursk region, an area south of Moscow and north of the Black Sea (an area larger than all of France). The Nazi

plan, known as Operation Citadel, called for German armies moving south from Moscow to meet with divisions moving north from Kuban, cutting off the salient from its command and supply lines. This would leave more than a million men and enormous quantities of material and provisions there for the taking. The strongest divisions were sent early in the summer with the best equipment and ample supplies; two hellish winters had taught the Wehrmacht many hard lessons about fighting the Russians on their home turf.

In spite of excellent intelligence (that Stalin ignored again and again), the Red Army was taken by surprise and failed to discern the Nazi plan even as the two prongs drew closer and the noose tightened. The plan demanded control of the air, and the Luftwaffe dedicated the bulk of its resources to securing the skies over Kursk. If successful, the plan was to establish defensible lines just outside Moscow, then dismantle the trapped Red Army, and hold that line while attending to the Allies in the south and west, after which the Wehrmacht would return to complete the conquest of Russia in 1944.

But then two things happened. First, a new plane rose to meet the 109s: the Yak-3. The fighter was as fast as any plane of the Luftwaffe and much more nimble, especially at low altitudes, where it insisted on doing its fighting. The Yak-3 could perform a complete 360-degree turn in 18.5 seconds at full speed, which made it deadly in one-on-one encounters with the Messerschmitts. For the first time, the Soviets could boast a better-performing aircraft than the Luftwaffe, and soon the Red Air Force established air superiority over the fierce tank battles being waged below.

A second factor also played a role in defeating the Luftwaffe. Large magnetite deposits in the mountains of Kursk played havoc with compasses and range finders. While German pilots were continually getting lost in the monotonous terrain, the Russian flyers, trained from the out-

Yak-3s were flown by units from several Allied countries. This one, known as *Yellow 24*, was flown by the French volunteer Normandie-Niemen unit.

set not to rely on instruments (because there weren't very many), used visual markings or sometimes even landed in battlefields to ask their comrades for directions. This made the careful planning that was the key to Luftwaffe operations nearly impossible, and further leveled the playing field in the battle for air control.

After only a week of intense fighting on the ground and in the air, it became clear that the Luftwaffe was not going to compensate for the Russian numerical superiority or the Red Army's tenacity. Claiming he was pulling troops out of Russia to defend against the Allied invasion of Sicily on July 10, Hitler ordered Operation Citadel abandoned. This time it was not the snow of the Russian winter or the desperate heroism of the Red Army that had thwarted Hitler; it was the clear superiority of a Russian weapon, the Yak-3. Instead of breathing a sigh of relief, the Red Army pressed the advantage it believed it had and began the counteroffensive that would ultimately lead the Red Army right to Hitler's bunker in Berlin.

The Yakovlev Department continued developing the Yak designs into faster and better-handling fighters well past the end of the war. Experts often point to the Yak-18, a two-seat trainer, as the ultimate in the series' design. The Yak-18 became celebrated as the favorite of cosmonaut Yuri Gagarin and was manufactured and sold in great numbers to air forces and flying clubs around the world for years after the war. It is safe to say that the Yak-18 won more international aerobatic competitions in the quarter century after World War II than any other aircraft in the world.

A design feature of the Yak series was the incorporation of an oil-cooling intake port into the wing at the wing-root. This, combined with the absence of avionic equipment, provided room in the Yak planes for the introduction of fuel and equipment needed for jet propulsion. Yakovlev was thus able to make the transition to high-performance jet fighters much quicker than even manufacturers in the West.

ABOVE: This squadron of Ilyushin Il-2 bombers is making one of the last bombing runs over Berlin in 1945. The Il-2 was one of many Soviet airplanes to incorporate design elements of the Yak series. LEFT: A two-seat trainer, the Yak-18, became the Soviet Union's premier training aircraft for the next generation of jet fighter pilots.

Chapter 16
The Dassault Mirage III (France)

The transition from propeller-driven aircraft to jet-propelled aircraft after the war was not an easy one. The jet engine, developed almost simultaneously in England and Germany, provided great power, but at a cost. Jet engines were extremely thirsty for fuel, which severely limited their range. The extra power allowed for bigger and heavier structures that could carry more fuel, but then new problems arose: aerodynamic forces and structural stress appeared in places and ways that baffled manufacturers. In spite of all the aerodynamic research that had been conducted by the United States, Britain, and Russia, only the Germans had a knowledge base of high-speed flight, meaning "transonic" or near the speed of sound, which is 761 miles per hour (1,224kph) at sea level and falls more or less uniformly to 660 miles per hour (1,062kph) at thirty-six thousand feet (11km). Much of the scurrying by the Russians and Americans to capture German scientists at war's end was directed to aerodynamic science as well as to rocketry.

The frenzied nature of the arms race between the United States and the Soviet Union resulted in a vast number of aircraft designs, and not a few deeply flawed jet aircraft went into production and were deployed in the 1950s and 1960s. In the area of commercial aviation, the consequences were sometimes catastrophic, as was the case with the de Havilland Comet. A design flaw in the fuselage caused a crash in May 1953 in which forty-three passengers died. The investigation that followed eventually revealed the flaw, and even though the problem was corrected, the crash effectively brought the Comet's career to an end, along with England's participation in the high-stakes business of large air transport manufacturing.

The fighter aircraft that were pitted against one another in the Korean War represented the results of the best research by both the United States and the U.S.S.R. The American F-86 Sabre and its

The Dassault Mirage III became a major French export and the backbone of many Third World air forces, often of countries belligerent toward one another. These two Mirages serve the Swiss Air Force.

RIGHT: These are several of Dassault's predecessors to the Mirage. From top to bottom: the Dassault MD-452-015 Mystere IIC, the Dassault Super Mystere IVB-1 prototype, and the Dassault MD Mystere IVB-03.

Soviet counterpart, the MiG-15, performed admirably in the skies over Korea, as did the next generation of fighters, the American Lockheed F-104 Starfighter and the MiG-17. But the finest-performing jet fighters produced in the early postwar decades came from France, which is remarkable considering how decimated the French aviation industry was by the end of the war (sometimes at the hand of Frenchmen who destroyed planes and equipment before fleeing the approaching Germans).

In 1937, a young aircraft manufacturer named Marcel Bloch watched helplessly as the French government nationalized the aircraft industry and took over his factory. He had hoped to have an important position in the new organization (SNCASO), and since his brother Paul was a high-ranking officer in the French army, he might reasonably assume this would occur. But Bloch was Jewish and unwelcome in the exclusionist French aviation community. When France fell, Paul, who was by now a general, became a leader of the underground; Marcel was arrested and deported to Germany (though he was a third-generation Frenchman). He spent two years in Buchenwald and just barely managed to survive the war.

In 1946 he returned to France and adopted the code name used by his brother during the war—Dassault—as his own and converted to Catholicism. The war had turned him into a driven man determined to make France a major air power so that it would never again be overrun. He applied the most exacting standards of engineering (and, since he was not about to see his company nationalized again, practiced the fine art of politics to a fare-thee-well).

The first product of the new company was the M.D.450 Ouragan, a jet fighter that showed the hallmark of all future Dassault planes: simplicity and reliability. The Ouragan became the initial mainstay of the Indian and Israeli air forces and established relationships between Dassault and those countries that would endure for decades. (The French soon came to understand that nations wishing for advanced fighter systems, but also hoping to remain nonaligned in the Cold War, would have to turn to producers other than the United States, the U.S.S.R., or even England for their future aircraft purchases.)

In 1952, the Ouragan had evolved into the Mystere IV, a truly supersonic jet that exhibited all the handling and performance requirements of transonic aerial combat. The Mystere was a major factor in the 1956 Sinai Campaign, though it was often up against a more powerful fighter, the Egyptian Air Force's MiG-15, supplied by the Soviet Union. As it became clear that the Soviets were going to commit their front line fighters to conflicts involving their client states, such as (at that time) Egypt and Pakistan, Dassault stepped up its development program to superpower status.

The result was the Mirage III, now produced by Dassault-Breguet, the basis for one of the jet age's most successful and prolific families of fighter aircraft. The Mirage I prototype was unveiled in 1955 and caused a sensation with its tailless delta configuration. Others had experimented with the delta wing, most notably Sweden's Saab in the development of the J35 Draken. The delta has many obvious advan-

tages: it allows for a stronger wing-root and hence lighter construction; there is significantly less drag; and, perhaps most important, the "drag profile" (that is, the surface the aircraft presents to the onrushing air) is minimized.

Its disadvantages are just as obvious: without a tail, there were no tail flaps to slow the plane down for landing and takeoff and no flaps to assist in turns. The more concentrated surface area of the delta also introduced two types of drag at high speeds as performance factors: induced drag (the cumulative resistance that builds as air flows across the wing surface) and trim drag (caused by the simple displacement of air by the bulk of the aircraft). Conventional wisdom in aeronautical circles was that these problems were insurmountable and would render the delta an undesirable configuration. But Dassault saw solutions to

RIGHT, TOP: The Mirage design was believed to be adaptable to other types of aircraft, such as this V/STOL (Vertical and/or Short Takeoff and Landing) Balzac V, unveiled in 1962. The airplane never reached full-scale production.

RIGHT, BOTTOM: In a 1957 test flight of the Mirage III, Roland Glavany took the aircraft to fifty thousand feet (15km), opened the throttle, and established a new speed record of 1,368.9 miles per hour (2,202kph), or Mach 1.8.

these problems through the use of sophisticated air brakes and super-reliable landing systems.

At the end of two grueling years of tests, the final version of the Mirage III was ready, demonstrating feather-touch agility at Mach 2. The Mirage III became the most sought-after piece of military hardware for the next twenty-five years. It became the core of more than thirty different air forces and was the key to the Israeli victory in the 1967 Six Day War. Thousands of Mirage IIIs rolled off the assembly lines, making France a world-class aviation producer alongside the United States, U.S.S.R., and Great Britain.

As if to prove the company was not wedded to the delta configuration, Dassault-Brequet unveiled the Mirage F-1 in 1966. It had a conventional wing and tail arrangement that used the basic (but much developed) Mirage fuselage. The F-1 was more maneuverable than the Mirage III, and although it had only half the combat radius of its predecessor (260 miles [416km]), its enhanced refueling capabilities more than compensated. In any event, the flight profiles of fighter sorties had changed radically in the late '60s. Fighters were not expected—or even permitted—to roam in search of engagement, but were sent to achieve specific objectives and then ordered to return. This cut down the range of the typical mission drastically.

The F-1 found many buyers with experience maintaining and flying the Mirage III, and kept France's forward position in military aviation. Then, as if to show its original devotion to the delta wing was not a momentary flirtation, Dassault-Breguet developed the Mirage further into the Mirage 2000, again a delta wing fighter, unveiled in 1978 and deployed in the early 1980s. The 2000 again utilized Mirage III sys-

LEFT, TOP: The Balzac, Dassault's short-lived V/STOL design, hovers over a French airfield in a 1962 test flight. LEFT, BOTTOM: The Mirage IV is capable of serving as both a conventional and strategic bomber.

tems and designs that had been developed steadily for more than twenty years. Many of the control problems presented by the delta could be solved, it was found, by advancing "fly-by-wire" (i.e., computer-controlled) avionics. With a top speed of fourteen hundred miles per hour (2,253kph), the Mirage 2000 was a worthy opponent of the most advanced American and Soviet fighters, even though their top speeds were about three hundred miles per hour (483kph) higher.

But this speed difference did not sit well with the French, so a second engine was added to the fuselage of the 2000, creating the Mirage 4000, a fighter with a maximum speed of two thousand miles per hour (3,218kph). This was more than a human pilot could handle; a Mirage 4000 coming out of a dive at two thousand miles per hour (3,218kph) would subject its pilot to 8 g's, or roughly the g-force encountered by an astronaut in a liftoff—but without lying prone and without special equipment. But at least the French could boast that the Mirage was still at the cutting edge of fighter technology.

To gain an appreciation of how successful the Mirage III (and the Mirage series) was, one need only consider how Dassault-Breguet and others took the basic Mirage design and adapted it to different needs, creating myriad top-of-the-line aircraft. The Israeli Air Force, the air force with the most combat experience with the Mirage, developed a fighter that took the Mirage III into the Mach 2 region. The Kfir was still an important fighter in the IAF in the 1980s when the American F-15 Eagle was introduced into the Israeli arsenal, a remarkable feat when one realizes the design of the Kfir is based on a twenty-year-old prototype. The IAF has gone on to develop the Lavie, based on what the Israelis have learned from both the Mirage 2000 and the F-15.

Meanwhile, Dassault-Breguet has applied "swing wing" variable geometry configuration in creating the Mirage G, a bomber-fighter escort that is more versatile than both the American F-111 and the Russian Tupolev Tu-26, and that is capable of being used as a strategic (i.e., nuclear weapons–bearing) bomber. The Mirage IV has become both a strategic and conventional bomber of choice for NATO and a dozen air forces. In fact, the Avro Vulcan B-1 strategic bomber has been the only non-American Western bomber with a range more than three thousand miles (4,827km) to challenge Dassault-Breguet in equipping the air forces of NATO. The clearest indication of the quality of the Dassault-Breguet aircraft—as well as French confidence in their product—is the fact that the French have been uncharacteristically insistent that NATO's procurement policy be based purely on objective criteria and not influenced by political considerations.

Chapter 17
The Hawker-Siddeley Harrier V/STOL Jet Fighter (U.K.)

The Hawker Harrier jet fighter is an aircraft that has persevered to become a great aircraft despite its many critics and detractors. The process has taken a long time—more than thirty years—and has involved many nations and manufacturers. Even the original British company, Hawker-Siddeley, has undergone radical changes, eventually becoming British Aerospace. Today, models of the Harrier are produced by McDonnell Douglas for the U.S. Marine Corps, as well as by the British and a pan-European consortium.

Historians point to the performance of the Harrier in the 1982 Falklands War as the test that proved the aircraft's quality, but this is misleading in two respects: first, the Harrier concept was clearly understood and appreciated by many builders of fighter aircraft long before the Falklands conflict (which explains attempts by the French, Americans, and Soviets to duplicate the British achievement); and second, even after 1982, the jury was still out on whether the Harrier is, or would ever be, a viable fighter aircraft, rather than just an oddity of aviation history.

The terminology for Harrier-type aircraft is "V/STOL," which stands for "Vertical and/or Short Takeoff and Landing" (as opposed to "CTOL"—"Conventional Takeoff and Landing"). Strictly speaking, this could apply equally well to helicopters and even airships, but the designation is used specifically for jet-powered or prop-driven airplanes. The Harrier had two forces that promoted it as a design concept: the first was the role Great Britain saw for itself in the community of aircraft manufacturers, particularly in military aircraft, and the second was the strategy that NATO was going to adopt in meeting the challenge posed by the Warsaw Pact nations and the Soviet Union. The story begins, however, with a detail in the origins of the jet engine.

When Frank Whittle invented the jet engine, he combined two forms of air compression then in use by gas turbines to create the air-fuel mixture that would then be combusted to produce a jet exhaust.

The Harrier represents one of the biggest and longest gambles in the history of aviation. Engendered by a British conviction that its industry's approach to jet propulsion was correct (or at least workable), several technological advances had to be made in order for the system as a whole to become a viable fighter.

One form is called radial compression (and the engine that uses it is known as a radial jet engine) and involves sucking air into the front of the engine and compressing it by pushing it outward with fans to the inner walls of the engine casing (nacelle). This compressed air is then moved to the rear combustion chamber, where it is mixed with fuel and ignited. The jet exhaust out the rear of the engine provides the forward thrust that moves the plane.

The intake air can, however, be compressed another way: by a series of fans that "sandwich" the air and move it along the length of the engine, each fan increasing the flow, and thus the pressure, until the air reaches the combustion chamber. This is known as an axial jet engine, because the airflow and compression take place along the long axis of the engine.

In the early days of jet engine technology, engineers debated which was the better approach. Each had its advantages and disadvantages. The radial engine was simple and had very few moving parts. It also had a high tolerance to heat and pressure, so it was easy to maintain. However, it also required a powerful engine, because most of the compression would be accomplished by the front rotors. The radial engine also required a larger opening through which to take in air, and a larger bulk for the rotors, which were using centrifugal force to push the air outward and compress it. (Hence the radial jet engine is also known as a centrifugal engine.) There was no easy way to transport the compressed air to the rear combustion area; it was just supposed to flow there, pushed by the incoming stream, but some of the compression energy was lost in leakage out the front.

The axial jet engine had many more moving parts and was prone to wear and breakdowns, but its drag profile was much smaller and thus more efficient. It compressed the air that moved through it in separate stages, so it was capable of generating more power, and most significantly, it did not rely on the intake stream to move the compressed air along to the combustion area; that was the job of the turbines. It was therefore not even necessary for the air to come from the incoming air stream; thus the engine could be operated efficiently from a standing start. Radial jet engines required rocket or prop boosters to get them up to a speed that would move the radially compressed air to the rear.

Whittle understood these relative virtues and drawbacks, and attempted to solve this by combining both forms of compression. The result was an engine that had the worst features of both: bulk, poor operation at low speeds, and complicated and fragile machinery. Amazingly, the Allied commanders ignored Whittle's invention, and his patent actually lapsed without any manufacturer showing any interest. In Germany, Pabst von Ohain was working (a bit later than Whittle, but independently) along similar lines, concentrating on the radial-flow engine for his employer, Ernst Heinkel. Heinkel successfully demonstrated the jet engine before the German High Command on July 3, 1939, and again in August, but received a cool reception that puzzled him. The Luftwaffe did not develop the jet aircraft until the outcome of the war was no longer in doubt.

This was an embarrassing turn of events for the Germans, but even more so for the British, who had, they felt, invented the jet engine. The clear advantages of the axial engine (today's jet engines are almost all axial in design) prompted a research program to iron out the bugs in the system. The British, believing they could not compete head-to-head with the Americans or the Soviets in aircraft manufacturing (a line of reasoning that eluded the French, with the result that they've competed very well with the superpowers), decided to concentrate their efforts on engine development, the crowning achievement of which would be the creation of an axial engine that would be able to power a V/STOL aircraft.

The second impetus for such aircraft involved a tactical matter in NATO defense. It was clear in the 1950s that the chief vulnerability of jet aircraft was their support facilities—airports, runways, fuel depots, machine shops, etc. Military aviation had become adept at bombing runways and incapacitating aircraft, and the speed with which Warsaw Pact bombers could strike and their proximity to NATO forces on the crowded European continent made the prospect of fighter aircraft that could be launched independently of runways and airports very inviting.

Both the French and the Swiss realized that this would give England a stronger voice in NATO, and each embarked on solutions of its own. The Swiss built runways and airport facilities inside mountains—fighters would literally take off from giant caves—but these still proved vulnerable to attack by chemical and even conventional ballistic weapons.

The French tried to develop V/STOL fighters of their own, but their approach was to create a "composite" system—one that used separate engines for lift and thrust. The result was the Dassault Balzac, a well-performing supersonic fighter that proved, however, to be too costly, too complicated and heavy, and not nearly versatile enough in the field. Never ones to bow out, the French followed up the Balzac with another composite V/STOL fighter, the Mirage III-V, capable of Mach 2, but with eight lift engines that all had to be working perfectly for the takeoff to go smoothly.

The Americans also tried their hand at V/STOL. The first approach tried was putting a jet on its tail and having it blast off. Aside from the difficulty pilots encountered operating an aircraft from a prone position, landing a plane vertically in rocketlike fashion proved a near impossibility (as a number of tragic tests demonstrated). The British approach, which was known as the "vectored-thrust" design, involved mounting an axial jet engine in the conventional way but directing its jet flow downward with swivel ports

The tactical capabilities of the Harrier are still being explored. One aspect of its field advantage is its ability to confuse enemy radar by showing the same radar signature as a helicopter.

on takeoff and then using the same ports pointing aft for horizontal thrust. The result was the Bell X-14, the first successful vectored-thrust V/STOL. But the design of the X-14 was seriously flawed: unlike more sophisticated jets, the engine had to be mounted in the front of the plane, which meant the plane's center of gravity was forward of the wing. There is a severe limit on how heavy such an engine can be, which places a severe performance limitation on the plane. American manufacturers have spent decades and many millions of dollars trying to perfect the vectored-thrust design; two failed designs include the Rockwell XFV-12A and the much-publicized Bell-Boeing V-22 Osprey. Finally, the U.S. Navy convinced the British to simply license an American company the right to produce the Harrier for use by the U.S. Marines and Navy.

The Russians also had a vigorous V/STOL development program, motivated mainly by their reluctance to place great reliance on aircraft carriers. Their Yak-38 Forger was developed as a naval fighter aircraft, but the vulnerability of aircraft carriers is such as to make carrier-based V/STOL aircraft of limited use. (If an aircraft carrier is successfully attacked, it does not mean simply that the runway surface is cut; the carrier sinks, and is thus of no use to any kind of aircraft.)

The British involvement with V/STOL began with a demonstration in 1953 of the Rolls-Royce "Flying Bedstead." The gangly design was calculated to highlight the reliance of the device on the two Nene turbojet engines, but the implications for both fighter and commercial aircraft were immediately obvious. The high lift-to-weight ratio engendered visions of commercial jet aircraft taking off from midtown "jet-pads" and transporting passengers by jet to distant cities. As fighter designs improved, the race was on: could Rolls-Royce develop their vectored-thrust engine and integrate it into a viable fighter design quickly enough to keep up with the fighter development accelerating because of the Cold War? Hawker had considered the need for CTOL fighter development as a prerequisite for the Harrier, and produced the Hunter, an excellent transonic fighter that was to serve as the eventual platform for the V/STOL engines once they were perfected.

The integration of the V/STOL system proved much more difficult than anticipated, and the program became a cornerstone of British military policy, almost bringing down several governments in England and Germany, which was a reluctant participant in the project. The early models were to be produced for both the RAF and NATO, the latter models designated the Kestrel, when Germany simply pulled out on the eve of production, leaving Great Britain alone in the V/STOL market.

When the British Aerospace Harrier GR Mk 1 and the rest of the series were finally unveiled in 1960, there were very few buyers willing to commit to V/STOL aircraft. The reason given most often was that the aircraft were designed to operate even after airfields were rendered

In tactical use, Harriers are well armed with air-to-air and air-to-ground missiles that give them the ability to conduct surgical strikes and close ground support while still being able to defend against conventional jet fighters.

unusable, but that would mean air superiority had already been lost, which would be catastrophic in any event. What good would Harriers do in that event? The most important underlying reason for poor sales, however, was that the lock the British had on the technology would make any customer wholly dependent on them for service, training, parts, and upgrades. The political ramifications were all too clear, and the Harrier, though a sensation at air shows and with great performance numbers, failed to interest many air forces around the world.

Then, in 1982, the Argentine government seized a small group of islands off its coast, the Falklands, that had belonged to Great Britain since colonial times. They were of little strategic or industrial value (there were many stories at the time of how there were more sheep on the island than people), but the Argentine government saw this as an opportunity to score points with its citizenry. Argentina also believed the islands were not defensible by England, and indeed they were not, since there was no British base within conventional bomber or fighter range.

The British, also regarding the matter as one of national prestige (and, as was later revealed, seeing this as a fortuitous opportunity to demonstrate the Harrier's capabilities), launched a military operation to regain the Falkland Islands. The tactic required the use of both land- and sea-based Harriers that would begin their missions in England, refuel in flight, and then carry out bombing runs on Port Stanley and Goose Greene. These strikes incapacitated the Argentine Air Force, and the British, operating from a well-camouflaged fleet of carriers and destroyers that served as landing platforms, eluded all attempts by the Argentine military to hamper their air campaign.

The British victory, seemingly tailor-made for the Harrier, ensured the success of the aircraft and led directly to the offer by the Americans to license its production. The Harrier came again to the attention of the public when it was a pivotal prop in the 1994 movie *True Lies*. The hero rescues a girl dangling atop a skyscraper by maneuvering a Harrier under her.

For aviation enthusiasts, the Harrier represents the fulfillment of the age-old dream of being able to fly at great speed and hover in one vehicle. The Harrier makes the need for mammoth aircraft carriers unnecessary, because a Sea Harrier is capable of front line fighter flight and can take off and land on a platform rigged to the deck of a standard-size cruiser. The Pegasus 11 jet engine, the key to the Harrier's performance, has been augmented by a PCB (Plenum Chamber Burning) engine that amounts to introducing afterburning in the vector vents of the engine, providing additional lift for the delicate maneuvers of takeoff and landing. After some thirty years, the U.S. Navy has finally accepted the pivotal role the V/STOL may play in a sea-based war and has outfitted an entire generation of ships and supersonic aircraft for the Harrier.

Chapter 18
The Boeing 707 (U.S.)

The story of the Boeing 707's creation has been told often: how the company gambled sixteen million dollars—a quarter of its net worth at the time—to develop the plane without a single order from either the military or a commercial airline; how the company kept the development of the 707 a secret (having learned its lesson when Donald Douglas used Boeing's publicity about the 247 to develop a better aircraft, the DC-3); and how the final development cost ballooned to a staggering $185 million, 20 percent greater than the company's entire net worth. Without question, the Boeing 707 was the greatest aviation gamble by a manufacturer up to that time. Douglas had spent a great deal on the DC-3, but the company would not have been driven into bankruptcy if the aircraft had failed; aviation people may be notorious risk-takers, but they are not (as a rule) foolhardy. Boeing, however, faced just such a fate if the 707 was to prove a dud. The newspapers reported, with a hint of criticism and a charge of irresponsibility, that the 707 project proved that high-stakes gambling was part of the personality of Boeing's president, William Allen.

A closer and less romanticized look at the story of the 707 shows that while it was true that Boeing faced ruin if the 707 failed to win a substantial number of customers, the decision to develop the plane was not made in haste or impetuously. Company records indicate that the meetings at which company executives discussed and debated whether or not to go ahead with the project ran into the thousands of hours. The advisability of building the plane continued to be discussed during the period of testing, which was itself a process that consumed many thousands of work-hours.

Bill Boeing, by then retired, wondered if Allen was taking the company he had founded down the road to ruin. But there were many executives and engineers at the company, people whom Boeing had hired and whom he respected, assuring him that the 707 was the plane of the future and that the gamble was worth taking. In company lore, the

The Boeing 707 bears the distinction of being the airplane that has found the most variations in the annals of aviation. The gamble by Boeing to recapture the commercial passenger aircraft market is one of the great episodes of American industry, as well as of aeronautical history.

ABOVE: The cockpit of the 377 is no less spacious than the rest of the plane, reminiscent of the great Clipper sea planes. **LEFT:** The Boeing 377 Stratocruiser was the land-based version of the great Clipper sea planes flown by Pan Am. The plane took the accepted aeronautical technology developed during World War II as far as it could go.

decision was said to have been made by Allen and Maynard Pennell, Boeing's director of development, at dinner the evening after the two had attended a demonstration of the de Havilland Comet at the Farnborough Air Show in 1950. In fact, though, the wheels had already been set in motion several years earlier.

The matter boiled down to three issues—three bits of information that Boeing searched out and nailed down—which, if resolved one way, would dictate building the plane. The first was an internal Boeing matter. The company had been the leading manufacturer of large bombers during World War II, having built the legendary bombers of the war, the B-17 Flying Fortress and the B-29 Superfortress. These planes had served remarkably well and established Boeing as the premier builder of large military aircraft. When the USAF decided to develop a jet bomber, it turned to Boeing and received the B-47 Stratojet, an adaptation of the 377 Stratocruiser passenger plane, a plane that Boeing had hoped would replace the DC-3 as the leading passenger aircraft, only to be outdone again by Douglas, who had developed the superior DC-6. Boeing had also extended the design of the B-29 to create the B-50, a prop-driven plane which the company believed would adapt well to jet engines when sufficiently powerful ones were developed. As that day approached (and as the Cold War got chillier), the air force approved the design for a long-range bomber that would combine the best features of the B-47 and the B-50; that plane was the B-52, which was also given the name Stratofortress.

RIGHT, TOP: The wind tunnel tests of the Dash 80 were among the most sophisticated conducted to that time, though the principle under which the researchers operated—gather all the information one can, whether it is relevant or not—came right out of the Wright brothers' notebook. RIGHT, BOTTOM: Wing construction and testing of the first Dash 80 prototype.

The speed and altitude characteristics of the B-52 would make it a bomber capable of reaching the Soviet Union with a single midair refueling, putting the plane in a class by itself. The B-52 series would eventually become the mainstay of the Strategic Air Command (SAC) of the USAF, but in 1950, it was still not equipped with sufficiently powerful jets. The executives at Boeing knew that the military was going to invest heavily in the development of advanced jet engines—the company that would be the major beneficiary of this investment was Pratt & Whitney. During the development phases of the 707, mock-ups of engines that did not yet exist, but which conformed to the specifications given to Boeing by Pratt & Whitney, were used in wind tunnel tests and in demonstrations. Donald Douglas became aware of the details of this program, but only much later, which was why he was so late getting into the race to build large commercial jet aircraft.

In addition to having knowledge of the government's jet engine program, the executives at Boeing took note of the fact that the effectiveness of the bombers they were supplying depended on the availability of refueling tanker aircraft that could fly nearly as high and as fast as the B-52s. No such aircraft were then available or contemplated, and in truth the air force was very late in coming to the realization that SAC's effectiveness required such support. There would be little threat posed from bombers that had to slow down and descend to a flight pattern that made them detectable and vulnerable to fighter attack close to enemy territory. When Boeing proposed developing a fast high-altitude tanker refueler, the air force rejected the idea, and much of the subsequent discussion at Boeing was the company's convincing itself that the air force would eventually come around.

The third piece of the puzzle was supplied by an exhaustive study conducted by United Airlines aimed at determining the future of air travel, specifically the role jet transports would play in that future. Beginning in 1952, and for more than a year, United operated a "simulated" airline—that is, an airline that had no planes, but kept schedules, encountered problems that had to be solved, and had phantom passengers whose responses to the performance and operation of the simulated airline were itself simulated on the basis of surveys and interviews with United's real-life passengers. The survey tested whether airports could handle the jet traffic and the extra business, whether jet travel would be accepted by the average air traveler, and if jet travel would find acceptance among the general public.

The conclusions of this survey became known to many airline executives, including the management of both Boeing and Douglas: the airports and the air-traffic-control system currently in place or being developed would be able to handle jet aircraft; air travelers clamored for the increased service offered by jet aircraft; and the greater range and speed would bring an enormous increase in the number of people who would consider air travel a viable option for long-distance trips, particularly overseas. United was not in a position to place any orders for jet aircraft before they were developed, the way TWA had placed orders for the DC-3 before the planes existed, even on paper. But the company kept in close touch with the two companies that were show-

ing interest in developing such planes, Boeing and Douglas, and was looking for the capital such a plunge would surely require.

So Boeing's frustrating history with commercial aircraft and the challenge posed by the de Havilland Comet may have influenced the company, but the decision to commit the company to the development of the 707 was made only after the company was certain all three parts

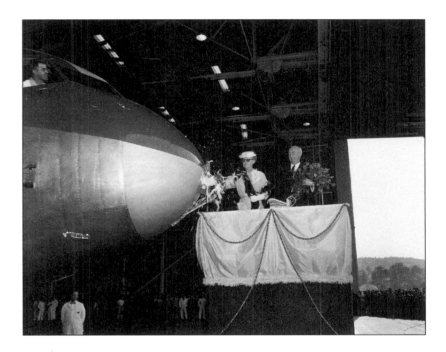

RIGHT, TOP: The christening of the Dash 80, renamed the Boeing 707, on May 15, 1954, by Bill and Bertha Boeing. **RIGHT, BOTTOM:** Aviation historians regard the building of the 707 as the fulfillment of the dream the Wright brothers had pursued more than a half century before.

of the puzzle—the engines, the need for a jet refueler, and the probable public support—had fallen into place.

The design of the 707 prototype, labeled the 367-80 to disguise the fact that it was a wholly redesigned plane, was headed by Edward C. Wells, the laconic chief engineer at Boeing who masterminded the entire 700 series, right up to the 747 Jumbo Jet. The "Dash 80," as it was called internally, went through the most exhaustive series of tests and design analysis of any aircraft to that time. The objective was not only to rethink the design of every element of the aircraft, but also to standardize every part of the airplane so that it could be constructed and maintained economically. Earlier aircraft models had some elements that were customized for each airplane. This was not going to be possible for a plane as large as the 707. Such latitude given to the mechanics in the shop and on the plant floor would turn out to be one of the causes of the weakness that resulted in the failure of the Comet's fuselage. At this level of aircraft building, nothing could be improvised; everything had to be the product of a blueprint and a specification. Each element of the aircraft underwent many hundreds of test-hours.

The first Dash 80 prototype produced was unveiled on May 15, 1954; Bertha Boeing shattered a bottle of champagne on the fuselage and a seventy-two-year-old Bill Boeing watched with a tear in his eye. The plane was a giant leap forward in aircraft design. The fuselage was reinforced with a titanium skeleton that would maintain its integrity even in the event of a breach. This was before the cause of the Comet's problems was determined to be structural weakness of the fuselage. (It was clear, however, even before the cause of the Comet crash of May 2, 1953, was determined precisely, that the fuselage structure was in part to blame.) The power plant consisted of four Pratt & Whitney JT-3 engines, mounted in four distinct nacelles under the wing. The Comet crash had reinforced public anxiety about jet engines built into the wings. In the B-52 design, engines were paired together into one mounting under each wing. The United survey had determined, however, that the public perception was that two jet engines in such close proximity were inherently dangerous. This was not the case (otherwise the configuration would not have been used on the bomber), but Boeing decided to bow to public perception.

RIGHT: One of the first 707s to undergo test flights. Some rival designers were surprised that the engines of the 707 were not built into the wings, but suspended below.

BELOW: Boeing has sold more 707s for military uses, such as the transports shown here, than for commercial uses.

The most advanced elements of the Dash 80 were in the wing design. The swept wing had a complex system of slats and flaps that could reduce the flying speed to less than 100 miles per hour (161kph). The wing also utilized "wet wing" configuration, in which the entire wing served as a fuel tank without extra casing for the fuel. Finally, the landing gear was the most advanced developed at that time, with a front center wheel assembly that retracted into the main fuselage. The plane underwent extensive flight-tests under the direction of Boeing's celebrated chief test pilot, A.M. "Tex" Johnston, whose input was critical to the ultimate design of the plane.

In spite of all the advances and successes of the Dash 80, it was not enough, and the plane was leading Boeing to another disaster. The reason was that Donald Douglas, though a latecomer to the race, was mounting a challenge that threatened to take the initiative from Boeing and maintain his preeminence in the field of commercial air transport. Douglas had concentrated on improving the design of the DC-6 and DC-7, the largest-selling passenger aircraft through the late 1940s. Once all the facts that had prompted Boeing to go ahead with the development of the new passenger jet became known, Douglas had to scramble to put together a design to compete with the Dash 80—with very little opportunity to test much of it.

The result was a remarkable airplane: the DC-8, a swept-wing jet that was faster than the Dash 80, thanks to an even newer engine developed by Pratt & Whitney, the JT-4, with greater power and efficiency, which in turn gave the plane greater range. Unlike the Dash 80, however, the DC-8 existed only on paper and as a model; the Dash 80 was a flight-tested aircraft. One might have thought that Boeing's lead was insurmountable, but United built a mock-up of the fuselage of each plane and put them side by side. The extra 16 inches (40.5cm) of the DC-8 so impressed the executives that they placed more orders for the DC-8 than for the Dash 80. When Pan American Airlines also ordered more DC-8s than Dash 80s, Boeing went back to the drawing board and reconfigured the aircraft. This would have been impossible were it not for the modular, standardized design that went into every element of the plane.

The outcome was the final version of the 707, only an inch (2.5cm) wider than the DC-8 but eight feet (2.5m) longer and thus able to accommodate up to twelve more passengers. The larger size and the integration of the JT-4 engines gave the 707 a range of nearly five thousand miles (8,045km), making it the first truly international air transport. The standardized design also permitted Boeing to reconfigure the aircraft in several sizes and outfittings so that airlines could order exactly the version that suited their particular needs.

The 707 became a wildly successful aircraft, setting a new standard for jet air travel, and becoming the model that has been adapted into the greatest number of variations of any aircraft ever produced.

The controls of the 707 were more sophisticated and complicated than those of any commercial aircraft produced up to that time, but pilots of the big bomber aircraft of World War II found many of the dials and controls oddly (and happily) familiar.

Chapter 19
The MiG-21 (U.S.S.R.)

The series of fighter aircraft that has been the mainstay of the Red Air Force in the post–World War II era—the period of the Cold War—has been the MiG series, named for the two principal designers of the aircraft, Artem I. Mikoyan and Mikhail I. Gurevich. The success of this series—and of one model in particular, the MiG-21 "Fishbed" fighter—can be attributed to a simple guiding principle that the builders and generals of the Soviet air force never compromised or forgot. The principle was that the essence of air superiority lies ultimately in the ability of a pilot in an aircraft to down an adversary aircraft. As the roles of Western fighter aircraft became confused and modified by the addition of new functions, such as serving as platforms for air-to-air and air-to-surface missiles, and as bomber support for ground troops, the question of air superiority was placed lower on the list of priorities. The Soviet Union suffered from no such confusion.

Momentary advances in NATO and American aircraft, particularly in the area of targeting avionics, gave the American planes brief periods of advantage in air engagements. It was the Soviet Union's steadfast adherence to the belief that these advances would eventually be countered, and the aircraft would again be matched in head-to-head combat, that informed the development of aircraft which handled spectacularly, even in the hands of pilots who were not well trained or suited to take full advantage of the aircraft's capabilities.

The Russian Design Bureau, the Soviet government agency in charge of fighter development, kept this priority straight and clear through three decades of fighter development by following several rules that typified MiG fighters, from the earliest postwar MiG-15 to the advanced Mach 3 MiG-25 "Foxbat" fighter. For example, the RDB always kept pilots intimately involved in aircraft development, assigning test pilots to the various design teams that would be responsible for different systems of the planes. In Western shops, pilots entered the picture later, and in American aircraft only at the very end when the

The MiG-21 "Fishbed" series of jet fighters proved a formidable adversary throughout the Cold War. Western military analysts liked to point out that the avionics of the Soviet fighter were on the primitive side, and that the engines were not very reliable, requiring much maintenance. But when the weather was good and the engines worked, they had to admit that the plane was more than a match for its NATO and American counterparts. The plane pictured here belongs to the Slovak Air Force.

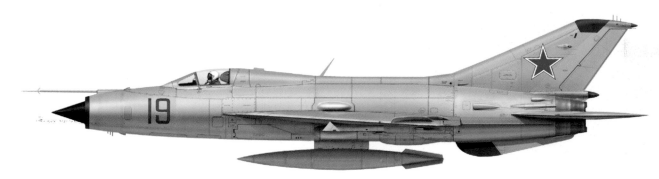

RIGHT, TOP: A MiG-21 of the Soviet
Air Force. Throughout the Cold War,
MiG-21s were frequently built under
contract by client states of the Soviet
Union. This meant that the design parameters of the plane had to be kept relatively simple, so that manufacturing
standards could be reached by less
technologically advanced countries.

RIGHT, BOTTOM: The F-86 Sabrejet
was the mainstay of the U.S. Air Force
in the Korean War, and in terms of pure
performance numbers it was outclassed
by the MiG-15. Only the superior training and ground support afforded the
U.S. pilots gave them an edge over
their adversaries in the Korean skies.

OPPOSITE: These MiG-21s are
equipped with missile pods on their
wings, indicating their possible use as
ground support fighters, but they were
rarely used for such high-risk sorties.

plane was ready for testing. The Western approach reflected a tradition
that owed much to the German aerodynamicists who looked to the laboratory and the wind tunnel to test their designs. Russians relied more
on input by the people flying the planes. There were things that pilots
knew about nuances of performance that eluded laboratory measure-
ment; thus, pilots were consulted even in areas of engineering in which
they had no formal training.

The Russians also believed the major focus of the pilot while flying an aircraft should be just that—flying. So systems that drew the
pilot's attention away from the flight of the aircraft were designed to be
as simple as possible and integrated into the ergonomics of flight control. Not that the MiGs were easy to fly. Pilots were expected to have
excellent flying skills, and trainer aircraft were often nearly up to the
flight characteristics of combat aircraft. It took many years for the
Soviets to allow the use of flight simulators in the training of pilots.
The belief was that the use of simulators promoted "soft" pilots who
would rely too heavily on instruments and not on their flying skills.
Western industry ascribed this reluctance to a failure in Russian technology, but later developments show this to be irrelevant, even if true.
The high accident rate of trainees when more advanced jet fighters
came along convinced the Soviets that simulators were necessary.

Finally, the Russian planes exemplified the Russian love of speed.
Every effort was made to give the MiG fighters as much speed as possi-

ble, even at the expense of other flight characteristics, such as maneuverability, ceiling, and range. All of these ideals had been a part of the
Russian aviation from its earliest days, and Mikoyan and Gurevich, protégés of Polikarpov, were well schooled in this tradition. The two
designers were not averse to using captured German aircraft and
plans—or even aerodynamicists captured after the war—to improve
their aircraft, but they never compromised on these traditions. The
result was a line of fighter aircraft that is arguably the most effective jet
fighter series in history.

The MiG series began with the MiG-3, unveiled in 1940. The
plane proved a disappointment against Luftwaffe aircraft, and it was
only the development of the Yak and Lavochkin fighters that saved the
Red Air Force. As a result of a major development program, the next
major MiG product was the MiG-15 jet fighter, called "Fagot" by
NATO, placed into service at the end of 1947. These are the planes
that fought in the Korean War, giving the American F-86 Sabrejets all
they could handle. In terms of pure flight characteristics, the MiG-15
was the better aircraft. But the plane was not easy to learn to fly, and
the American pilots enjoyed better training and better ground and aerial support. The initial engines used by the MiG-15 were British Rolls-
Royce Nene 2 engines—the loan of which strained relations between
the United States and Great Britain at the time—but soon the Russians
had developed adequate engines of their own. It was with the MiG-15

LEFT: A rare photo of three generations of MiG jet fighters together: from bottom, the MiG-15 "Fagot," used extensively in Korea; the MiG-21 "Fishbed" fighter, used throughout the Cold War; and the MiG-29 "Fulcrum," the Soviet response to the American F-15 fighter. **OPPOSITE:** It's now more than forty years since the MiG-21 fighter jet was first deployed, but the plane is still used extensively by many air forces.

that MiG surpassed Lavochkin and Yakovlev as the premier producer of Soviet fighters. The MiG-15 was produced in numbers greater, probably, than any fighter of the Cold War, and used in more air forces.

The West developed a number of high-performance fighters to outfly the MiG-15, most notably the F-104 Starfighter and the F-105 Thunderchief, but the chief rivalry of the next generation of fighter aircraft would be between the McDonnell F-4 Phantom series and the MiG-21 "Fishbed" fighters. Again, the superior Soviet aircraft suffered from the scarcity of qualified pilots, and the Phantom fighter, in the hands of the Israeli air force, for example, outfought the MiG-21s in most engagements, destroying a significant number of Egyptian MiG-21s while they were still on the ground.

The irony of the situation—that planes developed to the highest level of performance with the help of pilots were second in the field because there were not enough capable pilots to fly them—was not lost on the Soviets. In what was one of the odder developments in the history of aviation, the two superpowers traded development philosophies in developing the next generation of fighters. The United States began

concentrating on dogfight performance and pilot involvement in creating the F-15 Eagle, while the Soviets sought to mechanize the flight control in developing the MiG-25 Foxbat, thereby eliminating the great pilot input that had typified earlier designs. Both were formidable aircraft, but the F-15 has become the preeminent fighter of the last decade of the twentieth century, lending support to the earlier Soviet design values in fighter aircraft development.

In the hands of a capable pilot, however, the MiG-21 was an excellent aircraft, and its configuration allowed ever more powerful engines to be installed, upgrading the aircraft's performance several times through the 1970s. The fighter was capable of speeds up to Mach 2.1, with a ceiling of sixty thousand feet (18km) and a range of more than eleven hundred miles (1,767km). This made the MiG-21 a formidable fighter aircraft; in the minds of many experts, the MiG-21 reached the pinnacle in its class of fighter. It is no wonder that throughout the Cold War the MiG-21 was, more than all other Soviet aircraft, the one that the West most welcomed when a defecting Soviet pilot landed on American or NATO soil.

Chapter 20
The McDonnell Douglas F-15 Eagle (U.S.)

I n the 1970s it became clear that a new generation of fighters would have to be developed—ones that would combine the advanced electronic systems of the missile carriers and the dogfighting capabilities of the MiG and the Phantom. American fighters had undergone a transformation into the fighter-bomber role that the planes were called upon to fill during the Vietnam War. This led to the variable geometry configurations of the General Dynamics F-111 and the Grumman F-14 Tomcat. These planes had the capability of operating from aircraft carriers, which severely limited the performance of fixed-geometry aircraft, but offered safety that was not to be found in the air bases of Southeast Asia.

Then, in 1967, the Soviet Union developed a family of high-performance engines, the Tumansky R-series, and unveiled the MiG-23 interceptor fighter. The aircraft was powered by a Tumansky R-29 engine and was capable of Mach 2.2 for sustained periods, with a range of twelve hundred miles (1,931km) and a ceiling of sixty-one thousand feet (18.5km). These were formidable numbers that put the aircraft at the very top of the fighter field, but there was more coming. At an air show in Domodedoro near Moscow, the Red Air Force unveiled the MiG-25 "Foxbat." At first, Western analysts were skeptical about the capabilities of these planes, but all skepticism melted away when a model of the MiG-25 established new closed-circuit speed records for both five-hundred- and one-thousand-kilometer (310 and 620 miles) loops. Powered by the latest Tumansky R-31 afterburning turbojet engines, the Foxbat was capable of sustained periods at Mach 2.8, with a range of sixteen hundred miles (2,574km) and a ceiling of eighty thousand feet (24km). At that point, it was impossible for the Pentagon not to reevaluate its entire fighter program.

Such a study was undertaken in 1967 and was known as the "FX" (for "Fighter, Experimental") study. It included several of the compa-

Sometimes an aircraft is just plain lucky, as in the case of the F-15 Eagle. The plane's flight characteristics, along with its integration of weapons and electronics, have made the F-15 a favorite of top fighter pilots, even though other jet fighters have been developed with better numbers in one category or another. It is not surprising, then, that it is the plane used by the U.S. Navy aerobatic team, the Blue Angels.

The six control surfaces of the F-15 give the pilot a wide range of maneuvers that come in handy in dogfights with other fighters. The F-15 takes modular design to its ultimate extreme, making the aircraft one of the most operationally reliable fighters ever built.

nies then heavily involved in military aircraft construction in North America: Fairchild Hiller, General Dynamics, Boeing, Grumman, Lockheed, Ling Tempo Vought, and McDonnell Douglas. This stage of the project proved very difficult, as the old forces demanding that a fighter aircraft fulfill many functions kept being put forward. A concept paper issued by the USAF in September 1967 put an end to all the interservice bickering and established once and for all the character of the new fighter as an air-to-air interceptor that would have bomber and air-to-surface missile capabilities only as secondary functions. These flight characteristics were so stringent that competitors for the contract to build these planes would not be expected to produce prototypes for a fly-off. The decision would be based purely on reports on computer-generated and wind tunnel tests, which made not a few Pentagon officials uneasy.

The only company to survive this process was McDonnell Douglas. Under the direction of project manager Don Malvern, a page was taken out of the Soviet notebook, and company test pilots, under the general direction of chief test pilot Irving Burrows, were assigned to each of the system development teams. In an effort to avoid the huge cost overruns that had plagued the F-111 and C-5 Galaxy, a strict schedule of twenty-two milestone target dates were established for the development of the plane, now designated the F-15.

The first F-15 was rolled out at the McDonnell Douglas St. Louis plant on June 26, 1972. The plane was to undergo rigorous USAF testing at Edwards AFB. During the testing, an unknown USAF mechanic decided the wing needed to be shortened, so he crawled up on the wings of the multimillion-dollar investment with a hacksaw, cut off a slice from each wing, and filled it with wooden slats, to the horror of McDonnell Douglas engineers who witnessed the spectacle from the sidelines. Amazingly, the alteration improved performance, particularly in eliminating tail flutter at transonic speeds.

The first F-15 Eagles ready for USAF deployment rolled out at the end of the year and were in service by early 1973. Several innovations have made the F-15 the foremost fighter aircraft of the 1970s and 1980s. The power plant for the Eagle consists of two Pratt & Whitney F100-series turbojets, the configuration allowing for a steady development of more and more powerful engines. The F-15 is modularized as no other aircraft previously produced. Whole segments of the aircraft can be removed and replaced with other components without changing flight performance. The addition of panel access that allows maintenance crews to reach every part of the aircraft has brought downtime for the F-15 virtually to zero.

A feature of the F-15 that has increased performance in dogfight engagements is the variable-capture-area inlet ducts that automatically adjust to maximize air intake. This is particularly important in the close turns that typify dogfights. Finally, the F-15 has an advanced refueling system that is capable of taking on fuel in flight at fifty-five hundred pounds (2,497kg) per minute at high speed. This has greatly increased its combat effectiveness.

As always, the best (and, one might insist, the only) way the F-15 could be tested is combat. This opportunity came in the summer of 1990, when Iraq invaded neighboring Kuwait. Although the response was mandated by a United Nations resolution, most of the forces sent to counter this invasion were American. The military operation, termed "Desert Storm," pitted F-15s against Iraqi Mirage and MiG-23 and MiG-29 fighters. To the surprise of American intelligence, the USAF also encountered Iraqi-flown Sukhoi SU-17 fighters, advanced tactical fighters that were thought not to have been exported by Moscow. In these engagements, the F-15 showed its superiority as a fighter-interceptor, while most media attention was directed at the use of "smart bomb" laser-guided missile technology, a secondary function of the advanced plane.

The F-15 Eagle has become the main fighter of the Israel Defense Forces Air Force (IDFAF), which has used it to establish clear air superiority over Syrian MiG-supplied air forces. With the dissolution of the Soviet Union, Russia's fighter development program seems to have been halted, and the supplying of foreign air forces has become an expensive proposition that the Russian economy cannot support. This will directly impact the air forces of Arab nations that relied on a continued supply of modern fighters and parts to counter American-supplied IDFAF fleets. It now appears that the F-15 will remain the most advanced fighter into the next century. Even American development of an ATF—Advanced Tactical Fighter—has been slowed down in response to cutbacks in the Russian program.

ABOVE: Configured for two crew members, the F-15 Eagle seats the pilot in front and a weapons officer in the rear seat. **RIGHT:** The F-15's modular design ensures that it will remain viable for a long time to come, regardless of advances in engine design.

Chapter 21
The Concorde Supersonic Transport SST (U.K. and France)

The story of the Concorde SST is so enmeshed in the politics of the last half of the twentieth century that it is easy to lose sight of the fact that it represented a great achievement in aircraft design and manufacturing. Though I have tried throughout this work to avoid aircraft that stood alone, without other aircraft to which they could be compared, the Concorde will have to be an exception. Besides, one could argue that the Concorde did have a rival in the skies: the Tupolev Tu-144, nicknamed "Concordsky," was the Soviet entry into the supersonic sweepstakes. Though the Tu-144 never got beyond the test stage, its flight characteristics are known and can be compared to those of the Concorde. Moreover, an American SST was proposed by Boeing and got to at least the mock-up stage before the funding was unceremoniously withdrawn by Congress. (Today, the eleven-million-dollar model is a minor tourist attraction in Florida.)

In the early 1960s, four countries were looking to establish a credible presence in the sky as producers of commercial air transports. The United States had, by virtue of the Boeing 707 and 727, established a virtual monopoly in the market; French President Charles de Gaulle referred to "the American colonization of the skies" in assessing the situation. The British were getting over the setback of the Comet disaster and had developed the Trident 3, a tri-aft-mount-engined jet transport that carried 180 passengers—more than the 727—with great reliability. The Trident was built by Hawker-Siddeley, though the plane had been designed by de Havilland, indicating the turmoil in which the British aviation industry found itself in the post-Comet years.

The French had developed the SE-210 Caravelle, built by Sud Aviation and put into service in 1959. The twin-rear-engine design resulted in quieter cabins and greater flap area on the wings, which permitted shorter takeoffs and slower landings, both conducive to safety. The design inspired the designers at McDonnell Douglas, who built a virtually identically configured but larger plane, the DC-9, that stole

The SST Concorde represents a watershed in the history of aviation, where for the first time the economic and political realities of the modern world collided head-on with the capabilities of aeronautical technology. The question quickly went from "Can it be built?" to "Should it be built?"

Caravelle sales with its larger capacity.

The people at Boeing were not standing pat either. The 707 was being adapted to many different configurations, all of them superior to any of their European and American counterparts for ease of maintenance and for reliability. Boeing had by now established an incomparable worldwide sales organization that took up where Douglas had left off. The Europeans were even further behind in this all-important area of marketing than they were in aircraft development.

The Soviets had the furthest to go to catch up. The spartan appointments of Soviet aircraft, combined with the inefficiencies of the state-run Aeroflot airlines, made it impossible for the Russians to compete in any area of the globe other than behind the Iron Curtain. After many false starts and disastrous designs, the two main aircraft of the Russian commercial air transport fleet were the Tupolev Tu-114, a huge eight-engine turboprop that was among the fastest of its class ever produced, and the Ilyushin Il-62, an intercontinental jet with four engines mounted in the rear. The technical abilities of Soviet aircraft manufac-

turers was high, as witnessed by the strides being made in Soviet military aircraft, but years of neglect had made the Russians yearn for an opportunity to leap forward into the sweepstakes for international commercial aviation.

This was the environment in which Great Britain and France decided to join forces in entering the race to produce a viable supersonic transport. That it would require a huge investment by both governments was clear to all. The French and the British realized that sharing the costs would produce only a little savings for each. That the cost would be half of what one government would spend to develop the plane alone was purely for public consumption; there would have to be a great deal of duplication to allay suspicions and keep both countries happy, and the total cost would therefore be greater for the partnership. But England had had second thoughts about withholding its support and membership in the Common Market, and the French had similar misgivings about supporting British isolation from the European economic community. The Concorde was going to be an example of British-French cooperation, friendship, and trust, and would pave the way for eventual inclusion of Great Britain in the Common Market. With the requisite hoopla, the Anglo-French Supersonic Aircraft Agreement was signed on November 29, 1962.

From an aviation standpoint, two very capable designers collaborated on the design of the Concorde: Lucien Servanty of Sud and William Strang of British Aircraft Corporation. The two men chaired the team creating the basic design that would then be tested and perfected, and eventually become the Concorde. The wing design chosen was what is known as a double-delta (technically known as an "ogive"), which means a delta with a bend in mid-wing that softens the sweep. The design would allow the plane to cruise at Mach 2.2, or about 1,450 miles per hour (2,333kph), provided it cruised at an altitude of fifty thousand feet (15km). Any lower and the skin would heat up. Indeed, the Concorde is capable of still higher speeds, but its skin cannot handle the heat of friction, even in the very cold and thin upper atmosphere. The fuselage would have to be made entirely of heat-resistant titanium, which would add considerably to the cost. The delta wing was not the most efficient for supersonic flight, but it was the wing that permitted a reasonable landing speed. Even the Concorde's 177-mph (285kph) landing speed was faster than the Boeing 707's, and safe landing required a "feet-first" landing in which the plane descends tilted upward, lands first on its rear wheels, and is then lowered onto its forward landing gear. Tests have shown that passengers find this a nerve-racking experience, and feet-first landings are avoided whenever possible, but they would be standard on the Concorde. The landing also made it difficult for the pilot to see the runway (except by way of a television camera in the belly of the aircraft). To correct this, the plane was given a hinged mechanism that turned the nose and cockpit of the plane downward when landing.

The main problem with the Concorde was recognized almost immediately, and certainly before it was put into production: it was too small. The original model called for a passenger capacity of 118, but planes already in production carried up to twice that, and the Jumbo Jets being developed by Boeing—which would be produced as the 747—would carry four times as many passengers. It was clear that the limitation on passengers was going to be a problem: the cost of the airplane was going to be very high and the return limited, unless the fares were placed outside the range of the ordinary traveler. Last-minute attempts to enlarge the plane were unsuccessful; engineers determined that the five thousand testing hours that went into the smaller models would have to be scrapped and the development program begun from scratch, a possibility neither government found acceptable.

Naturally, fingers were pointed across the Channel; there was a growing demand for a scapegoat, and enough blame to go around. But the manufacturers, aware of how fickle governments and their constituencies can be, designed the program in such a way as to make both countries equally vulnerable. It would have been logical to divide the

The Concorde represented an attempt at British-French cooperation in a technical enterprise as part of a long-range plan involving the eventual unification of Europe. The problems encountered in creating an SST served the beneficial effect of alerting European leaders to some of the more intractable difficulties they would encounter as unification progressed.

work and, say, have one country develop the details of the wing and the other develop the engines. Instead, both countries worked equally on every element of the plane, so that when criticisms were raised, both countries were responsible for whatever went wrong—which certainly lowered the recriminations by a decibel or two.

The difficulty involved in developing the SST was underscored by the tragic crash of the Tupolev Tu-144, the Russian SST, at the Paris Air Show in 1973. In the accident, the plane came apart during a routine climbing maneuver; blew up, killing the crew of six; and crashed into a nearby village, killing seven on the ground. The Russian SST program never recovered, and the other models of the Tu-144 were soon mothballed. Meanwhile, the Concorde moved toward completion, while the number of advance orders dwindled in the face of the ballooning price.

Partly because of the Tu-144 crash (with the Russians out of the SST race, there was little reason for the United States to enter the fray), and partly because the Boeing design continually failed to meet airworthiness tests, Boeing abandoned the SST and concentrated on developing the 747. The plane was nearing completion in 1970 and was not without problems. The kinds of studies Douglas had conducted to see if American airports could accommodate the DC-3 were not conducted for the 747—and it turned out the airports were not ready. Baggage handling was overwhelmed, and food and other services were stretched to the limit, as were maintenance and fuel facilities. Most airports did not have long enough runways to handle the plane, and the gates and security were totally inadequate when the 747s began to fly.

Boeing was expecting these criticisms, and the only way it knew how to handle them was to focus on and point out the extraordinary measures to which it had gone to make the 747 the safest, as well as the largest, commercial jet in the sky. The structure (already enhanced by Boeing's titanium inner skeleton that made an in-flight fuselage breach virtually impossible) was made twice as strong as regulations required, and the wings were capable of handling 50 percent more stress than they would encounter in the most extreme conditions imaginable. Boeing also inaugurated an advanced training regimen for pilots, including special training on taxiing on the ground and an eighteen-wheel advanced landing gear configuration that used feet-first landing techniques for the wheel casings.

Still, it was not clear for some months after the plane was unveiled in 1970 whether the 747 would find buyers and passengers. Surprisingly (even to Boeing), the imposing appearance of the aircraft turned it into a prestige aircraft, and many national airlines felt compelled to have at least a few in their fleets as a matter of pride. In the end, the ability of the 747 to satisfy the need for prestige among airlines, a factor that had been crucial in the development of the Concorde, may have been the SST's undoing.

Whatever problems the 747 encountered, they were nothing compared to the Concorde's woes. Citizen groups organized to protest the noise, the sonic booms, and the air pollution of the aircraft, and many

Much to everyone's surprise, the Concorde is still in use, operated at a loss by a British-French consortium as a matter of prestige. Certain aspects of the plane that designers were worried about—its landing gear, for example—have not proven to be a problem, and the Concorde maintains a solid safety record. The maintenance program the plane requires, however, has become more expensive with time, making its future highly uncertain.

cities were considering banning SSTs from their airports, even in the rare instances where facilities could accommodate the plane. These protests never abated, even in the face of government action to promote the plane's operation in the United States. When the plane began test flights in 1972, its performance in the air was impressive, and it seemed that a hump may have been cleared.

By 1976, however, fourteen years after the project had begun, when the first Concordes were ready to be put into service, not a single one of the options taken from airlines other than British Airways and Air France became actual orders. In the end, these two airlines divided up the sixteen models built and operated them (at an annual loss) on the New York–London–Paris run purely as a matter of prestige.

There is no question that the Concorde represents a superlative in the aircraft designer's art. With its graceful lines along a body 204 feet (62m) long and a wing span of eighty-four feet (25.5m), the aircraft is still magnificent to behold, whether landing or in flight. On board, the planes have been luxuriously appointed, and today they hold between 100 and 108 passengers. The seats are a bit narrower than the standard seats of the 747, and the windows are very much smaller, but the time reduction is so great that passengers—usually business travelers who are crossing the ocean to conduct business and plan a quick return—do not seem to mind the cramped quarters.

The four rectangular-intake Olympus engines (also built jointly by England and France) under the wings together generate more than 150,000 pounds (68,100kg) of thrust. An interesting arrangement used by the Concorde is the system to pump unused fuel into auxiliary tanks in order to redistribute the weight of the plane as its thirty-four thousand gallons (128,690L) of fuel are consumed. As the twentieth century becomes the twenty-first, it is difficult to determine what will become of the Concorde models now in operation. The maintenance regime of the plane indicates that its outside envelope will be reached by 2006, though it is difficult to believe the planes will ever be mothballed.

In the meantime, not all was lost for the British and the French. In political terms, the Concorde accomplished its mission of ushering England into the European economic community. The Concorde even encouraged further cooperative ventures, this time with the Germans. The result was a formidable rival for the 747 (and, later, for the upcoming 777) markets: the Airbus A300.

Chapter 22
The Northrop B-2 Stealth Bomber (U.S.)

The development of the B-2 Stealth Bomber is clouded in secrecy—the plane existed and was flown for ten years before the United States acknowledged its existence. It was referred to (when referred to at all) simply as the ATB—Advanced Technology Bomber—and many millions of dollars were appropriated to its development by members of Congress who had not the vaguest notion of what it was. In fact, had President Jimmy Carter not needed to put teeth behind his claim that he was developing new weapons systems in the wake of the cancellation of the B-1 Bomber, the Stealth Bomber would probably have remained a mystery for another decade. As it is, if the B-2 falls victim to the budgetary ax—and with a price tag of up to half a billion dollars a plane, that may very well happen—it will be the second time the basic B-2 foundation design has been the victim of goings-on in Washington.

The design of the B-2 is based on a concept fathered by Jack Northrop a half century ago: the XB-35, or the Flying Wing. Based on a design he dreamed up in 1923, and given shape in the form of a balsa wood model built in his workshop, the concept was refined over the next quarter century as he worked out the aerodynamics of the configuration. By 1935, he felt he had solved most of the major problems, and he began building prototypes.

The early Flying Wing aircraft usually had some element designed to compensate for the absence of a fuselage and tail. Northrop admitted later that these elements were often added purely for psychological reasons: it seemed too much to ask of a pilot to accept a plane with nothing but a wing. But tests of the models created between 1929 and 1942 indicated that any deviation from the basic Flying Wing design sacrificed performance. The first truly all-wing aircraft, designated the N-9M, was flown in 1942 and was a scale model of the full-size XB-35 experimental bomber.

The B-2 Stealth Bomber proves, among other things, that the U.S. government can keep a secret when it really wants to. For nearly a decade, the Pentagon denied the existence of the B-2, hiding Congressional appropriations of billions of dollars in the budget and conducting tests in the California desert. The plane might have remained secret for many more years had it not become politically advisable for President Jimmy Carter to unveil it to the world.

In May 1947, Northrop delivered the Wilbur Wright Memorial Lecture, a prestigious annual event of the Royal Aeronautical Society in London. His topic was "The Development of All-Wing Aircraft," and he laid out the aeronautics behind the configuration, proposing several promising avenues of research. But the exploration of one such avenue was already well under way. In June 1946, the USAF had tested the first XB-35 Flying Wing bomber, and the results were very encouraging. The military saw immediately that the Flying Wing would adapt to the jet engine more readily than the prop-driven bombers the air force was currently deploying.

The transformation did not take long, because on October 21, 1947, the YB-49, a jet-powered flying wing 172 feet (52.5m) wide, took off from Northrop's test field in California. The test flights of the YB-49 demonstrated the excellence of the aircraft, and the air force placed an order for thirty aircraft to be used as advanced bombers to replace its aging B-36s, with the promise of ordering many more.

Then, just as suddenly, it seemed, the sale was canceled, after eleven of the planes were already built. There was no satisfactory explanation given at the time; the official explanation—that the planes were not suited for carrying atom bombs—was patently false, and everyone in the aviation industry knew it. Years later, it was learned that the air force had tried to use the contract to force a merger

LEFT, TOP: The ancestor of the B-2 was Jack Northrop's XB-35, the Flying Wing, at one time regarded as the most promising design for postwar bombers. **LEFT:** Few photos were published of the interior of the XB-35, but this photo, taken from the interior looking forward, indicates that the pilot and crew were afforded a surprisingly spacious cockpit.

Nine Flying Wings are parked dramatically at the Northrop testing grounds at Hawthorne, California. The sudden cutting of the program, only to see it resurrected in the Stealth Bomber, and the obvious adaptability of the XB-35 to jet technology have led some to speculate that the Flying Wing program had never really been scuttled, but that development was carried out in secret throughout the Cold War.

between Northrop and his chief competitor, Convair. The offer was made by Secretary of the Air Force Stuart Symington, who told Northrop that the deal for the YB-49s would be honored only if the two companies became one. Northrop refused and the entire project was scrapped, leaving Northrop with so bitter a taste that he retired from active participation in the company not long afterward.

It is likely that Northrop would have developed the Flying Wing into a commercial aircraft; he had mock-ups made of what the interior of such aircraft would be like. In his model, passengers would sit inside the wing facing the leading edge and watch the takeoff and flight through large full-length windows in the front of the wing. Compared to the restricted view passengers have on modern jet airliners, it is difficult to imagine what it would be like to ride in an airliner like the one Jack Northrop envisioned.

The Flying Wing remained a footnote in history for the next two decades or so, until the air force reevaluated the bomber component of

the "nuclear triad," the three delivery systems developed for the nation's nuclear arsenal (the other two components being ICBMs and submarine-launched missiles). The SAC's B-52 fleet was getting old, and the enemy's radar and intercept capabilities had improved vastly. In the early 1970s, the air force took a closer look at Low Observable (LO) technology, the official term for radar-evading stealth technology.

This technology was not new in the 1970s; it had been used in several aircraft as early as 1962. When the air force decided to develop a stealth bomber, it might have been expected to turn to the companies with the most experience in stealth technology, Lockheed and Rockwell. But the air force recognized that the Flying Wing configuration was crucial to the performance of the bomber, and the contract was awarded to Northrop. By the time the B-2 Stealth Bomber was publicly unveiled on November 22, 1988, it had already been flying around the secret testing area near the company's Palmdale, California, plant for nearly a decade.

The B-2 is considered the most sophisticated aircraft ever built (forgetting for the moment the space shuttle, which serves as both a vehicle for the exploration of space and as an airworthy glider), yet there is something elegantly simple about the aircraft. Flying through the air, it seems otherworldly, almost like a prop from a science fiction movie. Though its performance parameters are secret, it is known that it is powered by four General Electric F118-GE-100 turbofan jet engines, each capable of generating nineteen thousand pounds (8,626kg) of thrust. In the opinion of experts who are in a position to make educated guesses, this should give the B-2 a speed capability in excess of Mach 2. The control system for the B-2—both the control surfaces and the electronics controlling them—is the most advanced of any aircraft in the world (that we know about).

Yet the fate of the B-2 is uncertain as the twentieth century gives way to the twenty-first, and therefore its place among the list of great classic aircraft has yet to be decided.

OPPOSITE, TOP: This photo of the cockpit of the B-2 released by the USAF is an admitted fabrication, designed to give the public an idea of the level of sophistication of the plane, but no details of the actual controls. Such information remains classified. **LEFT:** This photo shows the split ailerons on the control surfaces of the B-2. A sophisticated computerized control system must work effectively to keep an aircraft like this stable without a tail rudder. **ABOVE:** Contrary to popular belief, the B-2 is not totally invisible to radar. It uses a combination of radiation-absorbing alloys and phantom radar beams to confuse enemy detection systems. Its computers permit it to fly very low to the ground, and it is capable of gliding without powered propulsion for long distances, making detection of its infrared heat signature difficult. The objective is not to be invisible, but to confuse the enemy until there is too little time to react effectively.

Index

Bibliography

Allen, Richard Sanders. *Revolution in the Sky*. The Stephen Greene Press, 1967.

Angelucci, Enzo, ed. *The Rand McNally Encyclopedia of Military Aviation*. New York: The Military Press , 1983.

————. *The Rand McNally Encyclopedia of Commercial Aviation*. New York: The Military Press, 1983.

Bowers, Peter M. *Boeing Aircraft Since 1916*. London: Putnam, 1966.

Braybrook, Roy. *V/STOL: The Key to Survival*. London: Osprey, 1989.

Brown, Arthur Whitten. *Flying the Atlantic in Sixteen Hours*. London: Stoke, 1920.

Caidin, Martin. *Me-109*. New York: Ballantine, 1969.

Chant, Christopher. *Aviation*. London: Orbis, 1978.

Coleman, Ted. *Jack Northrop and the Flying Wing*. New York: Paragon, 1988.

Combs, Harry. *Kill Devil Hill*. Boston: Houghton Mifflin, 1979.

Crickmore, Paul. *The F-15 Eagle*. New York: Smithmark, 1992.

Crouch, Tom D. *The Bishop's Boys*. New York: Norton, 1992.

Davies, R.E.G. *History of the World's Airlines*. New York: Oxford University Press, 1979.

Deighton, Len. *Fighter: The True Story of the Battle of Britain*. New York: Alfred A. Knopf, 1978.

Delear, Frank J. *Igor Sikorsky: His Three Careers in Aviation*. New York: E. P. Dutton, 1969.

Fenderburk, Thomas R. *The Fighters: The Men and Machines of the First Air War*. New York: Grosset and Dunlap, 1965.

Gilbert, James. *The Great Airplanes*. New York: Grosset and Dunlap, 1970.

Green, William, and Gordon Swanborough. *Great Fighter Aircraft*. London: Pilot, 1981.

Harris, Sherwood. *The First to Fly*. New York: Simon and Schuster, 1970.

Hegener, Henri. *Fokker: The Man and the Aircraft*. Fallbrook, California: Aero, 1961.

Holden, Henry M. *The Douglas DC-3*. Blue Ridge Summit, Pennsylvania: Aero, 1991.

Hooftman, Hugo. *Russian Aircraft*. Fallbrook, California: Aero, 1965.

Ingells, Douglas J., *The Plane that Changed the World*. Fallbrook, California: Aero, 1966.

Jablonski, Edward, *Airwar*. Garden City, New York: Doubleday, 1979.

Jablonski, Edward. *Atlantic Fever*. Garden City, New York: Macmillan, 1972

Lamberston, W. M. *Fighter Aircraft of the 1914–1918 War*. Fallbrook, California: Aero, 1964.

Lamberton, W. M. *Reconnaissance and Bomber Airctaft of the 1914–1918 War*. Fallbrook, California: Aero, 1962.

Lee, Asher. *The Soviet Air Force*. New York: John Day, 1962.

Macmillan, Norman. *Great Aircraft*. London: Bell, 1960.

Mason, Herbert M. *The Lafayette Escadrille*. London: Random House, 1964.

Mosley, Leonard. *Lindbergh*. New York: Dell, 1976.

Munson, Kenneth. *Airliners Between the Wars, 1919–1939*. London: Macmillan, 1972.

Penrose, Harold. *British Aviation— The Pioneer Years*. London: Putnam, 1967.

Robertson, B. *Sopwith: The Man and His Aircraft*. Seattle, Washington: University of Washington Press, 1970.

Roseberry, C. R. *The Challenging Skies*. Garden City, New York, 1966.

Ross, Walter S. *The Last Hero: Charles A. Lindbergh*. London: Macmillan, 1972.

Sciff, Barry. *The Boeing 707*. New York: Arco, 1967.

Serrano, Henry. *Contact! The Story of the Early Birds*. New York: Villard, 1987.

Sikorsky, Igor. *The Story of the Winged-S*. New York: Dodd, Mead, 1939.

Thetford, Owen. *Aircraft of the Royal Air Force Since 1918*. London: Bell, 1957.

Woodhouse, Jack. *The War in the Air, 1914–1918*. London: Almark, 1974.

Yakovlev, Alexander. *Notes of an Aircraft Designer*. Moscow: Foreign Language Publishing House, 1956.

Photography Credits